COLLABORATIVE, PARTICIPATORY, AND EMPOWERMENT EVALUATION

Also Available

Empowerment Evaluation Principles in Practice
Edited by David M. Fetterman and Abraham Wandersman

Collaborative, Participatory, and Empowerment Evaluation

Stakeholder Involvement Approaches

David M. Fetterman
Liliana Rodríguez-Campos
Ann P. Zukoski
and Contributors

THE GUILFORD PRESS
New York   London

Preface

As the field of evaluation continues to advance, there is a growing recognition of the need to build evaluation capacity for evaluators, program staff members, community members, and funders. Collaborative, participatory, and empowerment evaluation approaches make distinct contributions to evaluation practice. These approaches enhance capacity building and use by inviting and supporting participation of the multiple stakeholders in evaluation. Participation cultivates ownership and commitment, which has implications for follow-through and sustainability. Collaborative, participatory, and empowerment stakeholder involvement approaches to evaluation are guided by a profound respect for people and the ability of all to act and improve their own lives with the assistance and guidance of evaluators. However, there has been much confusion in the field about similarities and differences among approaches. Terms and definitions have been comingled and confounded. Some approaches are used in name only. This has led to some misapplications, reducing the value of and satisfaction with evaluation by its consumers.

This book provides needed clarity. It differentiates each approach from the others. It can assist evaluators as they select the most appropriate approach for the task at hand. In addition, this book can be a guide for community members and funders, ensuring that an appropriate match is made between the evaluation approach and the specific needs and resources of the community. This collection also represents an important contribution to the scholarly evaluation community, as it provides conceptual clarity and methodological specificity.

ORGANIZATION OF THE BOOK

This book provides an overview of each of the three approaches, along with definitions and case examples. Specifically, Chapter 1 provides an introduction to the various approaches, highlighting differences between them, based primarily on the role of the evaluator. The core of the book, Chapters 2–10, is designed to facilitate comparisons. The structure of the majority of the chapters consists of a definition, essential features, conceptual framework, advantages to using the approach, the role of the evaluator, guiding principles, and steps associated with applying each approach. Each approach is followed by two case examples.

The case examples range from an evaluation of an aquarium to that of a comprehensive sex education initiative. The settings and contexts range from corporate tech giants, such as Google, to nonprofits focusing on health improvement programs. This organization or format enables the reader to see how the "essentials" are applied in real life across stakeholder involvement approaches. Alternatively, the reader may simply want to read about the "essentials" of each approach, which provide enough information to enable the reader to be a more informed consumer.

Colleagues looking for greater clarity and guidance should take the time to read about the similarities across approaches in Chapter 11, focusing on principles in common. These principles are needed to guide an evaluation, particularly when navigating uncertain waters and new territories. For those who are trying to stay ahead of the curve, Chapter 12 is essential. It speaks to pioneering, and more seasoned, evaluators who are ready to push the edges of the envelope by combining approaches.

AUDIENCES FOR THE BOOK

Our hope is that this book become required reading in any evaluation course that is concerned with stakeholder involvement, building evaluation capacity, use, and evaluation sustainability. It can be used in any advanced evaluation course, focusing on collaborative, participatory, and empowerment evaluation approaches. The book is an excellent supplement to an introductory course, in which students will be engaged in evaluations that require stakeholder involvement in evaluation.

Practitioners will find the book helpful for selecting the most appropriate approach for the type of work in which they are engaged. In work with stakeholders, the book can provide guidelines for establishing realistic expectations, minimizing miscommunications concerning the level of stakeholder involvement, building evaluation capacity, and achieving desired results.

This book is also a "must read" for community members who want to become involved in evaluation and for funders of evaluation. It will help community members to become more informed consumers and reinforce the funder's role as an effective steward of philanthropic resources.

ACKNOWLEDGMENTS

The list of people, communities, agencies, and governments that have contributed to this collection is extensive. However, first and foremost, we thank the members of the American Evaluation Association's Collaborative, Participatory, and Empowerment Topical Interest Group. They represent much of the impetus for defining and differentiating approaches. In addition, they were the "playing field" for much of the development of these approaches, particularly at annual conferences. Special thanks are also extended to the two most prominent journals in the field for inviting and hosting much of the dialogue and critique that has shaped the approaches, specifically the editors of the *American Journal of Evaluation* and *Evaluation and Program Planning*.

We would also like to thank our domestic and international colleagues for their efforts applying these approaches in their communities. They have labored in the field of evaluation, posting problems and successes in blogs and on web pages, so that we might all learn from their practice.

Our students merit special consideration. They have added immensely to our insights and helped us clarify the intent of our communications. Their critiques and imaginative explorations and discussions about these chapters are greatly appreciated.

Finally, we thank C. Deborah Laughton, our editor at The Guilford Press, for understanding the need for this collection and supporting our efforts at every stage to bring it to fruition. The entire Guilford team has made this long-held dream a reality, and for that we give our thanks and appreciation.

We hope you find this volume engaging and an aid in your understanding and practice of evaluation. It is our hope that you find this knowledge helpful as you learn, teach, fund, and experience stakeholder-involvement approaches to evaluation.

Contents

An Introduction to Collaborative, Participatory, and Empowerment Evaluation Approaches

David M. Fetterman, Liliana Rodríguez-Campos,
Abraham Wandersman, Rita Goldfarb O'Sullivan,
and Ann P. Zukoski

Collaborative, participatory, and empowerment evaluations are stakeholder involvement approaches to evaluation. They have become increasingly popular over the last couple of decades.[1] They are being used throughout the United States and internationally. They address concerns about relevance, trust, and use in evaluation. They also build capacity and respond to pressing evaluation needs in the global community.

Over the past couple decades, members of the American Evaluation Association's (AEA) Collaborative, Participatory, and Empowerment Topical Interest Group (CPE-TIG) have labored to build a strong theoretical and empirical foundation of stakeholder involvement approaches in evaluation. Their efforts include identifying the essential features of collaborative, participatory, and empowerment evaluation. Defining and differentiating among stakeholder involvement approaches to evaluation serves to enhance conceptual clarity.[2] It also informs practice, helping evaluators select the most appropriate approach for the task at hand.

DIFFERENTIATING AMONG THE STAKEHOLDER INVOLVEMENT APPROACHES

AEA's CPE-TIG, composed of practicing evaluators from around the world, has endorsed this initiative and contributed to differentiating between collaborative, participatory, and empowerment evaluation. In addition, a long list of colleagues recommended that evaluation approaches to stakeholder involvement be differentiated (Miller & Campbell, 2006; Patton, 1997a, 2005; Scriven, 1997, 2005a; Sechrest, 1997; Stufflebeam, 1994), and many have helped to define and identify similarities and differences among these approaches (Fetterman, 2001a; Fetterman, Deitz, & Gesundheit, 2010; Fetterman, Kaftarian, & Wandersman, 1996, 2015; Fetterman & Wandersman, 2005, 2007; O'Sullivan, 2004; Rodríguez-Campos & Rincones-Gómez, 2013; Shulha, 2010; Zukoski & Luluquisen, 2002).

One essential way to highlight the difference between approaches is to focus on the role of the evaluator (see Figure 1.1):

- Collaborative evaluators are *in charge* of the evaluation, but they create an ongoing engagement between evaluators and stakeholders, contributing to stronger evaluation designs, enhanced data collection and analysis, and results that stakeholders understand and use. Collaborative evaluation covers the broadest scope of practice, ranging from an evaluator's consultation with the client to full-scale collaboration with specific stakeholders at every stage of the evaluation (Rodríguez-Campos & O'Sullivan, 2010).

- Participatory evaluators *jointly share* control of the evaluation. Participatory evaluations range from program staff members and participants participating in the evaluator's agenda to participation in an evaluation that is jointly designed and implemented by the evaluator and program staff members. They encourage participants to become involved in defining the evaluation, developing instruments, collecting and analyzing data, and reporting and disseminating results (Guijt, 2014; Shulha, 2010; Zukoski & Luluquisen, 2002). Typically, "control begins with the evaluator but is divested to program community members over time and with experience" (Cousins, Whitmore, & Shulha, 2013, p. 14).

- Empowerment evaluators view *program staff members, program participants, and community members as the ones in control* of the evaluation. However, empowerment evaluators serve as critical friends or coaches to help keep the process on track, rigorous, responsive, and relevant. Empowerment evaluations are not conducted in a vacuum. They are conducted within the conventional constraints and requirements of any organization. Program staff and participants remain accountable to meeting their goals. However, program staff and participants are also in

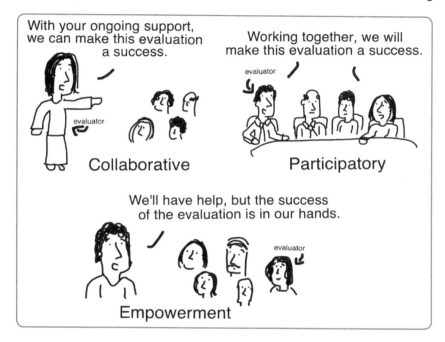

FIGURE 1.1. Comparison of stakeholder-involvement approaches to evaluation by evaluator role. From freshspectrum.com. Courtesy of Chris Lysy.

the best position to determine how to meet those external requirements and goals (Fetterman & Wandersman, 2010).

The chapters in this book are designed to help further distinguish one approach from another. The essentials of collaborative, participatory, and empowerment evaluation are presented in separate chapters in order to help practitioners compare and contrast approaches. In addition, case example chapters are used to illustrate what each approach looks like in practice.

COLLABORATIVE EVALUATION

The collaborative evaluation *essentials* chapter presents the definition, advantages, and essential features of this approach (see Chapter 2). The essential features focus on the Model for Collaborative Evaluations (MCE), a comprehensive framework guiding collaborative evaluation.

Components of the model include (1) identify the situation, (2) clarify the expectations, (3) establish a collective commitment, (4) ensure open communication, (5) encourage effective practices, and (6) follow specific guidelines. Chapter 2 also discusses collaboration guiding principles, the role of the collaborative evaluator, and specific steps to implement a collaborative evaluation.

Chapter 2 is followed by two case examples to demonstrate how the approach is applied. The first case example is a collaborative evaluation of an aquarium (see Chapter 3) that offers ecological and environmental stewardship education to the public. Programs for school students also include education about natural and human-induced threats to marine life. With over 80% of marine pollution originating from land sources (e.g., pesticides, untreated sewage), engaging students in learning environments such as Xplore! is essential to expanding their understanding about the causes and impact of pollution on marine life. In addition to pollution prevention, students in the Xplore! program learn about rescue, rehabilitation, and release for marine animals in distress.

The MCE is used to demonstrate the utility of this stakeholder involvement approach to evaluate an educational program about marine life. The chapter discusses the rationale for using a collaborative evaluation approach, including the development of a shared vision, sound evaluation, and improved outcomes. The chapter also highlights the interactive, supportive, and helpful nature of the relationship between the evaluator and the client in a collaborative evaluation.

The second case example is a collaborative evaluation of a multisite, multipurpose, multiyear early childhood Quality Care Initiative (see Chapter 4). Comprehensive, community-based programs for young children and their families have expanded over the past 20 years. These programs work with federal, state, local, and nonprofit organizations to integrate efforts in support of health and nutrition services, education, daycare and preschool centers, training of early childhood caretakers, screening and assistance for special needs students, literacy interventions, and parent education. In the Quality Care Initiative evaluated, 53 grantees provided multiple services to young children and their families in all these areas so that they would arrive at kindergarten ready to succeed. This is a critical contribution to our society. Over 60–70% of children younger than age 6 years regularly attend an early childhood program. "Children who attend high-quality early childhood programs demonstrate better math and language skills, better cognition and social skills, better interpersonal relationships, and better behavioral self-regulation than do children in lower-quality care" (Committee on Early Childhood, Adoption, and Dependent Care, 2005). Early childhood quality care is an investment in our future.

Chapter 4 focuses on four cyclical collaborative evaluation techniques applied to this early childhood Quality Care Initiative evaluation: (1) review program status, (2) develop evaluation plans, (3) implement the evaluation, and (4) share evaluation findings. This chapter also emphasizes the role of change, specifically organizational and programmatic change. The development of these childhood quality care programs required changes in almost every facet of their operations, from policies to personnel. Those who perform collaborative evaluations are accustomed to these transitions and understand that these programmatic changes require a continual adaptation of evaluation strategies to respond to client needs.

PARTICIPATORY EVALUATION

The participatory evaluation *essentials* chapter provides a definition of the approach (see Chapter 5). It also highlights two participatory evaluation streams: practical and transformative. It discusses the advantages associated with using each approach. Concerning essential features, Chapter 5 explains how participatory evaluation is based in part on an organizational learning theoretical framework. It also discusses the conditions required to conduct a participatory evaluation. The chapter's primary contribution, as it is in each of the *essentials* chapters, is the guiding principles. The evaluator's role and the steps required to conduct a participatory evaluation are also explored.

Two participatory evaluation case examples are presented in Chapters 6 and 7. Chapter 6 describes the use of a participatory evaluation approach to evaluate a community health improvement initiative, focusing on heart disease and Type 2 diabetes. There are over 1.5 million heart attacks each year. They are the number-one cause of death for men and women in the United States: one in three deaths are due to cardiovascular disease. According to the Centers for Disease Control and Prevention (CDC), heart disease and stroke cost over $316 billion in health care costs and lost productivity in 2011 (*https://millionhearts.hhs. gov/learn-prevent/cost-consequences.html*).

Approximately 9.3% of the population had diabetes in 2012. Type 2 diabetes occurs when the body can't use insulin properly. It is the seventh leading cause of death in the United States. The total cost of diagnosed diabetes was $245 billion in 2012 (American Diabetes Association, 2012). These two diseases alone point to the importance of these programs for our nation.

Chapter 6 presents the rationale for using a participatory evaluation. Multiple sets of stakeholders were engaged in the evaluation process of this community health improvement initiative, from planning through analysis and dissemination. The role of the advisory group was central to the evaluation, including the funder, the health system leading the project, and the evaluation team. This chapter also discusses specific steps, including (1) decide if a participatory approach is appropriate; (2) select and prepare an evaluation team; (3) collaborate on creating an evaluation plan; (4) conduct data collection and analysis; and (5) share results and develop an action plan. The synergistic relationship between program staff and the evaluation team is also described.

The second participatory evaluation case example presents an evaluation of a national, community justice program for high-risk sex offenders (see Chapter 7). This program was created in response to a significant problem that merits our attention. Approximately 20 million out of 112 million women (18.0% of the population) in the United States have been raped during their lifetimes (Kilpatrick, Resnick, Ruggiero, Conoscenti, & McCauley, 2007). According to Black and colleagues (2011), 81% of women who experienced stalking, physical violence, or rape by an intimate partner reported significant short- or long-term impacts. There are programs designed to respond to the needs of those impacted by sex offenders. In addition, there are programs designed to address sex offenders themselves. These latter programs provide concrete management strategies, from initial intake to community treatment programs (Abracen & Looman, 2015; Wilson, McWhinnie, Picheca, Prinzo, & Cortoni, 2007).

Chapter 7 discusses a participatory evaluation of a program designed to address high-risk sex offenders. It begins by reviewing participatory evaluation principles of practice, reinforcing the presentation of principles in the participatory *essentials* chapter. The chapter also describes the phases of the participatory practice: (1) creating an evaluation advisory/steering committee; (2) identifying an evaluation focus; (3) negotiating stakeholder participation; (4) evaluation planning and training;

(5) evaluation plan implementation; and (6) data analysis and interpretation. The role of the participatory evaluator, context, and equitable participation are also discussed.

EMPOWERMENT EVALUATION

The empowerment evaluation *essentials* chapter defines the approach and describes two streams, much like participatory evaluation: practical empowerment evaluation and transformative empowerment evaluation (see Chapter 8). The chapter discusses advantages of using the approach and presents its essential features. The conceptual framework is guided by empowerment and process use theory, as well as by theories of use and action. Additional features include the role of the critical friend, 10 principles, and specific empowerment evaluation approaches (three-step and 10-step approaches). Chapter 8 also explores the role of the empowerment evaluator or critical friend. It concludes with a brief discussion about the utility of an evaluation dashboard to monitor progress over time.

Two empowerment evaluation case examples are presented following Chapter 8. The first is an empowerment evaluation of a comprehensive sex education initiative (see Chapter 9). According to the CDC (2008), one in four young women between the ages of 15 and 19 has a sexually transmitted infection (STI). That is approximately half of the 19 million STIs reported each year. Approximately one person is infected with HIV every hour of every day in the United States (CDC, n.d.). Evaluations of comprehensive sex education programs demonstrate that these programs can (1) delay the onset of sexual activity, (2) reduce the frequency of sexual activity, (3) reduce the number of sexual partners, and (4) increase the use of condoms and contraceptives (see Kirby, 2007; Kohler, Manhart, & Lafferty, 2008).

Chapter 9 is an empowerment evaluation of a set of comprehensive sex education programs. It combines a three- and a 10-step approach to conducting an empowerment evaluation. It describes many of the changes that occur in an evaluation when an empowerment evaluation approach is adopted. Changes include, for example, *who* participates in the evaluation; *what* information is gathered and valued; and *how* information is handled and interpreted. Another notable point is how people change the way they think in an empowerment evaluation. Chapter 9 is also self-reflective, sharing lessons learned. Issues discussed include front-end demands and costs; rigor; reliability; use of theoretical models; pattern identification; communication; resistance; and outcomes.

The second case example is an empowerment evaluation of a doctoral program at Pacifica Graduate Institute. It was conducted by its own graduate students and their instructors (see Chapter 10). Students need to learn how to evaluate their own programs to prepare them for future roles in academic institutions and to contribute to their institutions' vitality. For example, accreditation requires self-evaluation and empowerment evaluation can be used extensively for precisely that purpose. Specifically, Stanford University's School of Medicine and the California Institute of Integral Studies have used empowerment evaluation to prepare for their accreditation reviews (Fetterman, 2012).

The use of the three-step approach to empowerment evaluation at Pacifica Graduate Institute was enhanced with technology and rubrics. These were provided courtesy of Google, which has developed a strategy for planning an evaluation using a series of worksheets and resources that we found can enhance empowerment evaluation.

A virtual classroom strategy, combined with the strategic use of online classroom management, rubrics, and evaluation programs, facilitated learning and enhanced use of the empowerment evaluation approach. Self-, peer-, and instructor assessments were closely aligned, highlighting the accuracy and validity of self-assessment. The triangulated evaluation approach also helped identify areas meriting attention and midcourse corrections. Lessons learned were reflexively mirrored back to Google to improve their evaluation capacity-building initiatives.

SIMILARITIES ACROSS THE THREE APPROACHES

Collaborative, participatory, and empowerment evaluation approaches have clear distinctions between them. However, there are many principles and practices that unite them. Chapter 11 presents the principles guiding each approach and highlights principles held in common. In addition to these principles, there are a great variety of other principles guiding stakeholder involvement approaches to evaluation. Organizing these principles according to macro-, mid-, and microlevels of analysis makes them more manageable and useful. In addition to principles, stakeholder involvement approaches to evaluation use many of the same methods and require similar skills, further demonstrating the similarities across approaches.

CONCLUSION

This collection concludes (Chapter 12) with a brief portrait of the international scope and practice of stakeholder involvement approaches to evaluation, including work in Africa, the Asian–Pacific area, Australia, the Caribbean, India, Indonesia, Latin America, Mexico, Nepal, Peru, the Philippines, southern Sudan, and Tanzania. In addition, collaborative, participatory, and empowerment evaluation approaches are applied to the same program (in a simulation) to illustrate the differences between the approaches, in terms of assumptions, roles, and community responsibilities. Chapter 12 also explores the potential utility of combining approaches (once one is familiar with both similarities and differences across stakeholder involvement approaches to evaluation).

The CPE-TIG leadership, represented by the authors in this collection, believes it is the nature of science and good practice to be precise, to define terms, and to explain differences among similar approaches in order to build on knowledge and improve practice. Differentiation of approaches helps evaluators select the most appropriate stakeholder involvement approach in the field. The more informed that the evaluator, funder, and program staff and participants are, the more meaningful, relevant, and useful the evaluation. Together, these chapters contribute to conceptual clarity, help demystify evaluation practice for practitioners, and build evaluation capacity.

NOTES

1. The CPE-TIG represents approximately 20% of the membership.
2. This view of science and practice is presented in response to the comments of Cousins et al. (2013) about differentiating among approaches (p. 15).

CHAPTER 2

Essentials of
Collaborative Evaluation

Liliana Rodríguez-Campos

Collaborative evaluation is practiced in the United States and in many countries around the world, such as Brazil, Chile, China, Costa Rica, Ecuador, Korea, Puerto Rico, Saudi Arabia, Spain, and Vietnam. It has been applied to a wide variety of settings, including business, nonprofit, and education (Rodríguez-Campos, 2015). In the last decade, collaborative evaluation has grown in popularity along with similar approaches, bringing together evaluators and stakeholders from different disciplines and cultures to exchange knowledge on how collaboration can be used as a strategic tool for fostering and strengthening evaluation practice (Rodríguez-Campos & Rincones-Gómez, 2017). This approach has an increasing number of supporters and has benefitted immensely from feedback by colleagues (e.g., Arnold, 2006; Bledsoe & Graham, 2005; Cousins, Donohue, & Bloom, 1996; Fetterman & Wandersman, 2007; Gajda, 2004; Gloudemans & Welsh, 2015; Green, Mulvey, Fisher, & Woratschek, 1996; Guerere & Hicks, 2015; Martz, 2015; Morabito, 2002; O'Sullivan & Rodríguez-Campos, 2012; Ryan, Greene, Lincoln, Mathison, & Mertens, 1998; Scriven, 1994; Stufflebeam & Shrinkfield, 2007; Veale, Morely, & Erickson, 2001; Yeh, 2000).

DEFINITION

Collaborative evaluation is an approach in which there is a substantial degree of collaboration between evaluators and stakeholders throughout the process to the extent that they are willing and capable of being involved (e.g., Cousins et al., 1996; O'Sullivan, 2004; Rodríguez-Campos, 2005; Rodríguez-Campos & Rincones-Gómez, 2013, 2017). Collaborative evaluators are in charge of the evaluation, but they create an ongoing engagement between evaluators and stakeholders.

ADVANTAGES

Collaborative evaluation is an approach that offers many advantages, such as access to information, quality of information gathered, opportunities for creative problem solving, and receptivity to findings. This approach distinguishes itself in that it uses a sliding scale for levels of collaboration, for each different evaluation will experience different levels of collaboration. For instance, the range can be from an evaluator's consultation with a client to a comprehensive collaboration concerning all phases of an evaluation (planning, executing, and reporting). Collaborative evaluation assumes that active, ongoing involvement between evaluators and stakeholders results in stronger evaluation designs, enhanced data collection and analysis, and results that the stakeholders understand and use. A collaborative evaluation fosters personal, team, and organizational learning (Morabito, 2002).

ESSENTIAL FEATURES

Collaborative evaluation's essential features include its conceptual framework, principles, roles, and specific steps. These features provide an insight into the nature of collaborative evaluation. (A more detailed description is provided in Rodríguez-Campos & Rincones-Gómez, 2013.)

CONCEPTUAL FRAMEWORK

The Model for Collaborative Evaluations (MCE)[1] is a comprehensive framework for guiding collaborative evaluations in a precise, realistic, and useful manner (Rodríguez-Campos, 2005, 2008; Rodríguez-Campos & Rincones-Gómez, 2013). This model has a systematic structure and revolves around a set of six interactive components specific to conducting collaborative evaluations, providing a basis for decision making. The MCE helps to establish priorities in order to achieve a supportive evaluation environment, with a special emphasis on collaboration. The MCE has been used in multisite and multiyear evaluations, at the national and the international level, and for both formative and summative purposes.

Figure 2.1 provides the conceptual framework for viewing the MCE components interactively: (1) identify the situation; (2) clarify the expectations; (3) establish a collective commitment; (4) ensure open communication; (5) encourage effective practices; and (6) follow specific guidelines. Additionally, each of the MCE subcomponents, shown as bullet points in the outer circle of the figure, includes a set of 10 steps suggested to support the proper understanding and use of the model. The implementation of the MCE has been very effective because it is possible to make adjustments during execution as well as to immediately recover from unexpected issues such as the extent and various levels of collaboration required throughout the evaluation.

Each of the MCE components influences the others and, as a consequence, the overall collaborative evaluation. Even though the MCE could create the expectation of a sequential process, it is actually a system that incorporates continuous feedback for redefinition and improvement in which changes in one element affect changes in other parts of the model. To accomplish a comprehensive collaborative evaluation, the interactive use of the MCE elements on a rotating and remixing basis is recommended. However, new insights, and associated benefits, may be gained by using each of the model components individually as well.

Identify the Situation

The situation is a combination of formal and informal circumstances determined by the relationships that surround and sustain the collaborative evaluation. It sets the foundation for everything that follows in the evaluation. This component of the model also considers issues related to the applicability of a collaborative approach to ensure it is appropriate given the current situation. The evaluation situation represents an early warning signal, highlighting potential constraints and benefits (e.g., funds, staff, materials, and time needed to support the collaboration process) associated with the collaborative evaluation. It can help evaluators better manage the effort and anticipate any potential barriers.

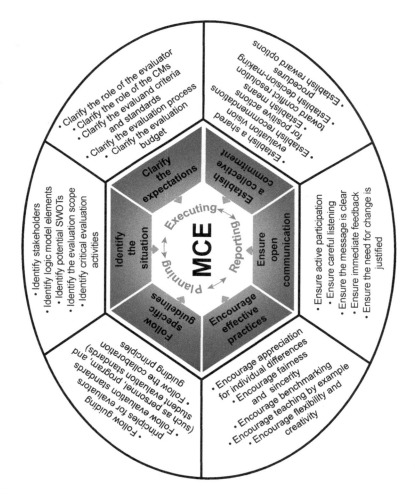

FIGURE 2.1. The Model for Collaborative Evaluations (MCE). From Rodríguez-Campos and Rincones-Gómez (2013). Copyright © 2005, 2013 Liliana Rodríguez-Campos and Rigoberto Rincones-Gómez. All rights reserved. Used by permission of the publisher, Stanford University, *sup.org*.

This MCE component is divided into the following five subcomponents: (1) identify stakeholders, (2) identify logic model elements, (3) identify potential SWOTs (strengths, weaknesses, opportunities, and threats), (4) identify the evaluation scope (e.g., evaluation questions, work breakdown structure), and (5) identify critical evaluation activities.

Clarify the Expectations

An expectation is the anticipation that good (or bad) may come out of the collaborative evaluation. It is the assumption, belief, or idea we have about the evaluation and the people involved in it. A clear expectation is very important because it influences all the decisions made during the evaluation. By clarifying the expectations, everyone understands which issues must be addressed and what the best ways are to achieve desired results in order to make effective contributions. As a result of clarifying the expectations, it is possible to understand the implications of each evaluation choice made. In addition, a control process can be followed to show whether evaluation activities are being carried out as planned.

This MCE component is divided into the following subcomponents: (1) clarify the role of the evaluator, (2) clarify the role of the collaboration members (CMs), (3) clarify the evaluand criteria and standards, (4) clarify the evaluation process, and (5) clarify the evaluation budget.

Establish a Collective Commitment

A collective commitment is a compromise to jointly meet the evaluation obligations without continuous external authority or supervision. In a collaborative evaluation there is a need for this type of commitment in order to promote a desire to take responsibility and accountability for it. Through a collective commitment, the evaluator and the CMs gain a sense of ownership of the effects of this process and its commitment to continuous improvement. This increases awareness and the willingness to make adjustments to enhance the quality of the collaborative evaluation. Love and Russon (2000) stated, "evaluation will remain one of the world's best kept secrets unless we build strong coalitions that go beyond our own backyards" (p. 458).

This MCE component is divided into the following subcomponents: (1) establish a shared evaluation vision, (2) establish recommendations for positive actions, (3) establish means toward conflict resolution, (4) establish decision-making procedures, and (5) establish reward options.

Ensure Open Communication

Communication is a process of social interaction (such as speaking, listening, or writing) used to convey information and exchange ideas in order to influence specific actions within the collaborative evaluation. Both formal (evaluation-related) and informal (personal) communication strategies must be planned to reflect the diverse styles of the collaborative evaluator and the CMs (and other stakeholders) within the collaborative evaluation. Effective communication involves understanding others as well as being understood oneself (Gibson, Ivancevich, & Donnelly, 2008). Thus, it is important to foster a group dialogue of openness and exploration that continues among the CMs themselves (even outside formal meetings).

This MCE component is divided into the following subcomponents: (1) ensure active participation, (2) ensure careful listening, (3) ensure that the message is clear, (4) ensure immediate feedback, and (5) ensure that the need for change is justified.

Encourage Effective Practices

Effective practices are sound, established procedures or systems for producing a desired effect within the collaborative evaluation. Among other ways, it can be accomplished by balancing evaluation resource needs. Also, fostering an atmosphere in which everyone is supportive of everyone else's capabilities increases recognition that each individual provides important input to the evaluation process. As a result, people feel empowered and able to actively interact in the collaborative evaluation activities because (e.g., by focusing on strengths) there is a belief that each contribution makes a difference.

This MCE component is divided into the following subcomponents: (1) encourage appreciation for individual differences, (2) encourage fairness and sincerity, (3) encourage benchmarking, (4) encourage teaching by example, and (5) encourage flexibility and creativity.

Follow Specific Guideliness

Guidelines are principles that direct the design, use, and assessment of the collaborative evaluations, their evaluators, and their CMs. Guidelines provide direction for sound evaluations, although they alone cannot guarantee the quality of any collaborative evaluation. By identifying and addressing where the collaborative evaluation meets the necessary guidelines, the evaluator(s) and the CMs demonstrate a clearer understanding of what the process is about and how it should be carried out. If adopted and internalized, these guidelines may serve as a baseline for the collaborative evaluators and the CMs to use and improve them.

This MCE component is divided into the following subcomponents: (1) follow guiding principles for evaluators, (2) follow evaluation standards (such as program, personnel, and student evaluation standards), and (3) follow the collaboration guiding principles.

The greatest strengths of the MCE are that it gives focus to collaborative evaluations and a strong basis for establishing long-term relationships. This model provides information on how to build collaborative relationships within an evaluation, while recognizing that the level of collaboration will vary for each evaluation. It is a tool that helps everyone involved to better understand how to develop priorities and achieve a high level of support within a collaborative evaluation. According to Sanders (2005, p. iii), "The model, based on the author's experience and extensive reading, serves as a guide for evaluators who believe that making evaluation an integral part of everyday work in programs and organizations is important." (There are also other collaborative evaluation frameworks that can be used and adopted, including the collaborative evaluation techniques discussed in Chapter 4.)

PRINCIPLES

Collaborative evaluation is shaped and influenced by the Collaboration Guiding Principles, which are established tenets that guide the professional practice of collaborators (Rodríguez-Campos & Rincones-Gómez, 2013). The principles are implicitly present throughout a collaborative evaluation, helping to blend together the six MCE components. They represent the diversity of perceptions about the primary purpose of collaboration and guide its everyday practice. Hence, they are conceptualized here as general ideals or expectations that need to be considered in collaborative efforts. They include (1) development, (2) empathy, (3) empowerment, (4) involvement, (5) qualification, (6) social support, and (7) trust. They are briefly described below:

1. *Development* is the use of training (such as workshops or seminars) or any other mechanism (e.g., mentoring) to enhance educational learning and self-improvement.

2. *Empathy* is the display of sensitivity, understanding, and a

thoughtful response toward the feelings or emotions of others, thereby better managing a positive reaction to your collaborative environment.

3. *Empowerment* is the development of a sense of self-efficacy by delegating authority and removing any possible obstacles (such as feelings of inadequacy) that might limit the attainment of established goals.

4. *Involvement* is the constructive combination of forces (such as strengths and weaknesses) throughout the collaboration in a way that is feasible and meaningful for everyone. The level of involvement varies among everyone who collaborates in the effort.

5. *Qualification* is the level of knowledge and skills needed to achieve an effective collaboration. It is the preparation for dealing with relevant performance issues that are directly affected by the individual's background.

6. *Social support* is the management of relationships with others in order to establish a sense of belonging and a holistic view of social-related issues. It is the ability to develop productive networks in order to find solutions in a collaborative way.

7. *Trust* is the firm confidence in or reliance on the sincerity, credibility, and reliability of everyone involved in the collaboration. Although a high level of trust must exist for a successful collaboration, trust takes time to build and can be eliminated easily.

Evaluators continuously benefit from guidelines developed by various associations regarding appropriate activities that need to be followed and met. The Collaboration Guiding Principles together with other guideliness (such as the AEA's Guiding Principles for Evaluators) direct the design, use, and assessment of the collaborative evaluations; their evaluators; and their CMs. They provide direction for sound evaluations, a clearer understanding of what the process is about, and how it should be carried out.

ROLES

There are a set of actions expected from the evaluator(s) and the CMs in terms of what needs to be done in a collaborative evaluation. The evaluator accepts responsibility for the overall evaluation and its results, employing defensible criteria to judge the evaluand value. The CMs are specific stakeholders (possessing unique characteristics) who work jointly with the evaluator(s) to help with particular tasks in order to achieve the collaborative evaluation vision.

The roles in a collaborative evaluation are multifaceted, and everyone involved is required to have a mix of strong conceptual, technical, and interpersonal skills. Everyone's role should be clearly defined, without being overly restrictive, to avoid overlap with the evaluator(s)' and other CMs' roles. In addition, roles should be suited to everyone's interests, skills, and availability. (See Rodríguez-Campos & Rincones-Gómez, 2013, for a more detailed description of the roles of the evaluator and CMs.)

STEPS

There are many ways by which to implement a collaborative evaluation. The MCE serves as an iterative checklist that provides consistent step-by-step guidance for the collection of relevant evidence to determine the value of the evaluand. Specifically, each of the MCE subcomponents includes a set of 10 steps suggested to support the proper understanding and use of the model. (See Rodríguez-Campos & Rincones-Gómez, 2013, for a traditional formulation of such a checklist.) For example, the following steps are suggested to *identify potential SWOTs*, which is a subcomponent of *Identify the situation* in Figure 2.1:

1. Create a SWOTs matrix on a flipchart (poster or other similar option) and have available a variety of color-coded, self-adhesive cards (such as blue for strengths, yellow for weaknesses, green for opportunities, and red for threats).

2. Review relevant data (e.g., historical information on this and other evaluands) to have some examples that could be identified as SWOTs, such as technology and information availability, assigned budget, and time considerations.

3. Divide the participants (including CMs and other stakeholders as needed) into four teams representing strengths, weaknesses, opportunities, and threats. Then provide each team the color adhesives identifying their particular SWOT.

4. Instruct each team to write one specific idea per adhesive, under their specific team SWOT, until they run out of ideas. Then the

team leader will read to their members each of the ideas and, with their feedback, eliminate any overlap.

5. Place the color adhesives on the flipchart, under the specific team SWOT, so the rest of the teams can read them. In the case of the opportunities and threats, only leave those that have at least a 50% chance of occurrence.

6. Invite participants to make note of their new ideas about the SWOTs (to make sure all the most important ideas are addressed) and share each of those ideas while adding them to the SWOTs matrix as appropriate.

7. Ask for ideas or feedback from other stakeholders who may help identify additional realistic SWOTs (such as unintended results or areas that may have been overlooked). Then question every alternative before adding it to the SWOTs matrix.

8. Agree with all the participants and other specific stakeholders, as feasible, on a definitive SWOTs matrix. This final version of the SWOTs matrix should be clearly aligned with the evaluand vision and mission to understand which issues deserve attention.

9. Design with the participants' emergency procedures (e.g., risk analysis, predefined action steps, or contingency plans) and plan for timely feedback throughout the evaluation to provide early warning signs of specific problems.

10. Gather feedback on a regular basis using a previously agreed-upon system, such as meetings, and summarize it in a written format (including an updated version of the SWOTs report) so it is available to each CM and other stakeholders as appropriate.

The MCE steps have a wide potential applicability for conducting collaborative evaluations because different aspects will have greater relevance in certain cases depending on specific contextual factors. Each set of steps can be visited individually as needed because they are easy to follow and allow for quick guidance. For example, each program evaluated will have its own unique group of people, interests, and disagreements. Thus, the steps for the subcomponent *Establish means toward conflict resolution* could be more relevant in one evaluation than in another. The MCE provides an important learning opportunity on how to conduct collaborative evaluations step by step.

CONCLUSION

Optimal use of collaborative evaluation requires awareness of its strengths and weaknesses, its proponents and detractors, and any potential opportunities and threats along the path of implementation (Rodríguez-Campos, 2012b). Furthermore, the effectiveness of an evaluand is increased when the knowledge, responsibility, and action required to meet its goals become unified. Thus, through collaborative evaluation, it is possible to achieve a holistic learning environment by understanding and creating collaborative opportunities. In such an environment, stakeholders better understand the evaluation process and are therefore more likely to use its findings.

Collaborative evaluation is growing, as evidenced by new literature, presentations, and discussions. There is room for improvement as collaborative evaluation develops over time. For instance, the CPE-TIG has available an interactive blog and a Google collaborative Web page to provide additional opportunities to enhance dialogue and reinforce lessons learned among collaborative evaluation practitioners. As collaborative evaluators continue to share their experiences, including chapters such as this one, the approach will continue to be more refined and effective.

NOTE

1. This section abstracts material that is presented thoroughly in *Collaborative Evaluations: Step-by-Step* (2nd ed.) (Rodríguez-Campos & Rincones-Gómez, 2013).

CHAPTER 3

A Collaborative Evaluation of an Aquarium (Marine Life Program)

Liliana Rodríguez-Campos, Rigoberto Rincones-Gómez, and Rosalyn Roker

The purpose of this chapter is to provide readers with a better understanding of how a collaborative evaluation approach can be used to evaluate an educational program intended to increase primary-grade-level students' understanding of marine life. The MCE (Rodríguez-Campos & Rincones-Gómez, 2013) was described in Chapter 2. It is one of the most common collaborative evaluation frameworks and will be used here to demonstrate the utility of this approach. This chapter provides readers with an introductory overview of the program evaluated, the rationale for our decision to use a collaborative approach, how the various components of the MCE were applied in the design and implementation of the evaluation, and a summary of our findings and conclusions.

THE PROGRAM

Xplore! Marine Life (hereafter Xplore!)[1] is a summer program designed to teach elementary school students about various forms of marine life and the many natural and human-induced factors that may pose challenges to it. This program is funded by a nonprofit aquarium; over 100 students from both private and public schools participate in Xplore! every summer. Program instructors apply different instructional methods, including the use of technology, to teach students about marine life. The program integrates instruction and activities similar to those of the school curriculum (e.g., reading, mathematical computations, physical movement, and hands-on activities), in addition to promoting collaborative interaction as students work together to identify different forms of marine life and threats to their survival. The goals of Xplore! are to enhance students' knowledge of (1) marine life and human-induced and natural factors that might pose challenges for marine life, (2) rescue and rehabilitation protocols for certain distressed marine life, and (3) the relative size of marine life compared to the vast and dynamic ocean.

WHY A COLLABORATIVE APPROACH?

Utilizing a collaborative approach for this evaluation allowed pooling everybody's individual strengths and collectively building a relationship with relevant key stakeholders. Incorporating stakeholders in the evaluation process facilitated access to important information and provided a resource to better understand situations that might arise during the evaluation. Additionally, the engagement of evaluators and stakeholders together lent itself to the creation of a shared vision. This increased the likelihood of a sound evaluation, conducive to improved overall outcomes.

The MCE is a framework that can be used by evaluators to systematically guide collaborative evaluations in a precise, realistic, and useful manner. This model, which has six interactive components, provides a basis for decision making and helps establish priorities to achieve a supportive and productive evaluation environment. It also has an emphasis on elements that facilitate collaboration.

Using the MCE, the evaluators and stakeholders were able to build useful communication channels. In addition, the model helped identify potential concerns resulting from involvement in the evaluation. The MCE also helped access information and identified the need for professional knowledge, prior to, during, and/or after the evaluation was conducted. Moreover, a collaborative evaluation oftentimes does not include all members of the program being evaluated. In these instances, the MCE provides an avenue to amass organization-specific knowledge necessary for a comprehensive evaluation through the creation of a team of CMs.

Building a collaborative evaluation team inclusive of the evaluators and organizational representatives enhances the credibility of everyone's skills and expertise necessary for collection and analysis of relevant information for the evaluation. When a group of CMs work collabora-tively during the evaluation process, different perspectives can be con-sidered and incorporated, if appropriate, leading to minimal opportunity for biased results.

APPLICATION OF THE MCE

The MCE includes a set of checklists for use by the collaborative evalu-ation team. They were used, for example, to ensure that all stakehold-ers in Xplore! had a shared commitment to the evaluation process, that their expectations were clear, and that communication remained open (among other elements essential to conducting a sound evaluation). The use of the MCE in an educational program that teaches children about marine life can increase the likelihood of more comprehensive evalua-tion practices (Wharton, 2015). When the MCE is employed, evaluators and key stakeholders are actively engaged, leading to a sound evaluation. Listed below is an illustration of how the six components of the MCE can be implemented in evaluations of a marine life educational program.

Identify the Situation

We met with several members of the aquarium's education department management staff, after receiving information that they were interested in having some of their programs evaluated. The senior education man-ager was identified as the specific client for the purpose of the evaluation. Stakeholders for this evaluation included the aquarium's executive man-agement staff and board members, the Xplore! program's staff members, and local school teachers.

The program was marketed to local elementary schools as a sum-mer program for students. Program registration was contingent upon the schools scheduling trips for students. Registration rates fluctuated for a variety of reasons, including weather conditions and lack of enough stu-dents eligible to attend. This was an important issue, as one of the goals of the client was to learn how the aquarium could grow the program's rate of registration. Understanding the client's desires and needs early on helped us to identify which stakeholders should become CMs. The client and five members of the education department were identified as most knowledgeable about Xplore! and best suited to collaborate during the evaluation process.

The first meeting with the CMs took place in early spring. Based on the estimated amount of time required to gather pertinent information for the evaluation, we agreed to schedule the final evaluation report to be completed by late fall. Then, the collaborative evaluation team (evaluators and CMs) would present the evaluation results to the client in time to make adjustments prior to the beginning of the upcoming summer sessions. In addition to presenting the final report, we agreed to provide progress notes at least twice during the evaluation process. This allowed the client to make immediate adjustments to the program instead of having to wait until the final report was issued.

We had an opportunity to meet several education department staff members and program instructors, and to tour the entire facility during our first meeting. The client presented information on Xplore!, and expressed concern about the sustainability of the program. This also led to a detailed discussion of other reasons for the client making a decision to have the program evaluated.

A major strength for the XPlore! evaluation process was that all of the resources needed to conduct the evaluation were in a central location. The classrooms were at the aquarium, and the students and teachers were required to attend the sessions on-site. For preparation purposes, the participating schools were required to provide advanced notice to Xplore! staff of how many students and teachers would be in attendance each day. On a few occasions, last-minute cancelations and "no shows" occurred, which negatively impacted XPlore! revenue.

Xplore! was relatively new and the aquarium was interested in boosting its visibility and opening the program to students year-round. In addition, the client indicated that the aquarium's education department was interested in expanding its program offerings to target the same audience and wanted feedback that could not only help enhance Xplore!, but potentially be incorporated into future program developments. In order for us to have an idea of what was needed for the evaluation and to create a timeline for deliverables, it was imperative to identify the critical evaluation activities.

Clarify the Expectations

When the expectations are clarified, everyone involved in the collaborative evaluation understands which issues should be addressed and seeks the most effective ways to achieve the desired results. Clarifying expectations contributes to a sense of ownership, enhances confidence, and increases productivity. Overall, it can help to cultivate a harmonious working relationship among the collaborative evaluation team. Clarifying expectations can also help people anticipate the impact of decisions made during the evaluation process.

Our meeting included a discussion about the CMs' and evaluators' roles, anticipated needs, and responsibilities during the evaluation process. We emphasized that recommendations for improvement were welcomed throughout the evaluation process. To ensure that everyone was on the same page and knew what was expected of them, we explained what the collaborative evaluation entailed. We gathered information about the individual CM's qualifications and listened carefully to identify their individual expectations. We then provided a description of each CM's role in the evaluation and, with their approval, assigned them roles that were most suitable to their qualifications and expectations. In doing so, we believe this action maximized the CM's individual potential, stimulated motivation among CMs, and was instrumental in producing a sense of shared ownership for the collaborative evaluation.

The evaluand criteria and standards were clarified after the client solidified the evaluation questions. An evaluation plan, including a timeline for the evaluation, was formally delivered to the client after it was clear that all the CMs involved in the process were in agreement with the evaluation. For instance, we clarified and provided detailed descriptions of expected activities to be completed during the planning, execution, and reporting phases of the evaluation. The plan was modified early during the evaluation process after we discovered that important information was not being captured. We notified the client and made the appropriate adjustments to the plan.

Establish a Collective Commitment

One of the key components of a collaborative evaluation is establishing a collective commitment among the collaborative evaluation team. When the CMs are actively involved in the evaluation process, they become more committed to the evaluation and feel a sense of connection. Additionally, the CMs' commitment is enhanced when their contributions to the evaluation are acknowledged and recognized.

Everyone involved in the collaborative evaluation was able to develop and maintain positive relationships. In addition to motivating the team to remain focused on the evaluation purpose, the shared vision created collaboratively helped meet the evaluation obligations without continuous supervision. A collective commitment produced a desire to take responsibility and accountability for the evaluation. A collective commitment to this evaluation also motivated the client and CMs to make a slight modification of the program delivery to assist with capturing essential information during observation of attendees that otherwise would not have been possible. In addition, they ensured that program instructors and other staff members provided us with the assistance needed to complete the evaluation.

Ensure Open Communication

Communication is an important part of a collaborative evaluation. Formal and informal lines of communication require continual attention and assistance. Open lines of communication provide stakeholders with an opportunity to exchange ideas, improve decisions, share feedback, and make modifications to the evaluation, as needed.

The MCE supported our open and timely exchange of information with the CMs. Throughout the evaluation process, we maintained open communication and engaged in dialogue on a regular basis to discuss concerns, needs, and results. When not on-site conducting observations of Xplore!, our primary mode of communication was by e-mail and phone. The mutual respect among the collaborative evaluation team allowed everyone to have candid conversations about the evaluation findings. We rarely encountered a delay in any request for information.

Our open lines of communication encouraged the CMs to learn more about the evaluation design and procedures. It also helped to reduce anxiety and concerns among CMs. By focusing our attention on CMs' concerns, we were able to address potentially adverse effects on the quality of the evaluation.

Maintaining open communication also helped to identify potential problems throughout the evaluation process, to take appropriate action in a timely fashion, and to receive suggestions for improvement. We found this feedback useful to both understand and validate our need to make adjustments during the evaluation. The needed changes were a result of unforeseen time constraints with accessing program participants. To maximize how much information we could gather from Xplore! participants, we had to modify how and when we distributed questionnaires. In addition, we needed assistance from the instructors with prompting students to respond to a question related to the program objectives. We recognized that the original design of the questionnaire did not allow us to capture that information. These adjustments were beneficial to the outcome of the evaluation and caused neither a delay or inconvenience.

Encourage Effective Practices

Xplore! was a relatively new program that had never been evaluated. Therefore, the evaluation plan had to be designed from scratch since no previous plan was in place. The collaborative evaluation team had diverse personal and professional backgrounds. This allowed all of us to pool our individual strengths to conceptualize an evaluation proposal that would allow capturing information aligned with the needs and interests of the client. We received full support of the CMs and client to complete the evaluation.

Because of the logistics of the program and our dependence on the client to provide scheduling information for program participants, the collaborative evaluation team had to remain flexible. An example of highlighting our flexibility occurred when less than half the students who were registered for the program showed up for a session. The Xplore! instructors indicated that there were not enough students to run the traditional concurrent sessions. Thus, all students were combined into one group, resulting in observations of the same set of students throughout the entire program session.

Another example of being flexible during the evaluation of the Xplore! program occurred when teachers informed us that they did not have time to answer our questions at the end of Xplore! sessions because they had to monitor their students. We knew that in order for us to capture needed information for the evaluation, we had to come up with another way to get the teachers to complete the evaluations. With the assistance of the program instructors, we asked teachers if they would complete our questionnaire as they accompanied their students through the hour-long program sessions instead of at the end of the sessions. In this way, we were able to obtain more detailed and comprehensive information than we would have been able to obtain had we asked the teachers the questions at the end of the session.

Because of our diverse backgrounds and experiences, it was essential for everybody involved in the evaluation to embrace opinions and styles that were not the same as what they were accustomed to throughout the process. Fortunately, there was a lot of cohesiveness among the collaborative evaluation team, which made instances of disagreement few and far between. This was important because the client and the CMs were the experts in Xplore! operations and were able to proactively recognize potential issues that we might encounter throughout the evaluation.

Follow Specific Guidelines

Although guidelines alone cannot guarantee the quality of evaluations, they are helpful in providing sound direction. This MCE approach is comprised of three subcomponents—(1) follow guiding principles for evaluators, (2) follow evaluation standards, and (3) follow the collaboration principles—all of which should be used to help guide the collaborative evaluation team.

We incorporated the guiding principles for evaluators, which include (1) systematic inquiry, (2) competence, (3) integrity and honesty, (4) respect for people, and (5) responsibilities for general and public welfare in every aspect of the evaluation process (American Evaluation Association, 2004). These principles were essential because they helped ensure that our results were trustworthy and less likely to be biased. In addition, we followed the evaluation standards (Joint Committee on Standards for Educational Evaluation, 2003, 2009, 2011), which guide the design, implementation, assessment, and improvement of an evaluation. Being versed in the standards increased the likelihood that the collaborative evaluation team would conduct a sound quality evaluation. Lastly, the collaborative evaluation team followed the seven collaboration guiding principles, including (1) development, (2) empathy, (3) empowerment, (4) involvement, (5) qualification, (6) social support, and (7) trust, which represent diversity of perceptions about the primary purpose of collaboration. These principles proactively guided the collaborative practice of the evaluation. Everybody involved in the evaluation received training on these guidelines to ensure they had a clear understanding of them prior to conducting the evaluation.

ADDITIONAL COMMENTS

This evaluation formatively determined the extent to which the program expanded students' knowledge of marine life and teachers' perceptions about the program. A collaborative approach was best suited for this evaluation as it promoted open lines of communication, clear expectations, and a collective commitment among the collaborative evaluation team, which was essential to the evaluation success. The client was very responsive to requests made throughout the evaluation and updated the collaborative evaluation team with information such as schedule changes as soon as was possible.

An example of the client's responsiveness took place when we initially began observations of students' participation in Xplore! and encountered difficulty capturing some data that was vital to determining the students' understanding of information presented by the program's instructors. We notified the client of that obstacle and recommended a possible solution, which entailed a minor adjustment to how and when instructors posed questions to students throughout the program presentation. The client accepted the recommendation, which led to a slight modification to the program delivery by Xplore! staff. Commitment to the evaluation was also evidenced by the timely exchange of information with the client, and the swift adjustment in the program delivery by Xplore! instructors.

Another example of the clear expectations and collective commitment was evidenced by the readiness of the Xplore! instructors to inform teachers, chaperones, and students that the evaluators were present to observe the program. The brief introduction was also intended to clarify any questions that teachers and students may have had about the observations. It appeared to lessen barriers between the evaluators and teachers, which was helpful with data collection. Initially, we approached teachers toward the end of the sessions to ask if they were willing to complete a survey related to their perception of Xplore! Primarily due to time constraints and the responsibility of monitoring their students, the teachers did not have sufficient time to complete the surveys. After communicating this issue with the client, we changed our strategy and began approaching the teachers at the beginning of the sessions and requested that they return the completed surveys to us at the end of the sessions. We were available during the sessions if the teachers had any questions related to the surveys, and this change in procedure resulted in almost a 100% participation rate in survey completion. As a result, we were able to capture very detailed information related to the teachers' perceptions of Xplore!, including whether they would recommend the program to other teachers. The collaborative approach used to conduct this evaluation enhanced the efficiency and effectiveness of data gathering, as well as the accuracy of the results.

CONCLUSION: LESSONS LEARNED

The MCE is an appropriate model for guiding the evaluation of an educational program designed to teach primary grade students about marine life. We confirmed how important it is for the collaborative evaluation team to have a shared vision and to feel that their contributions are valued; also, the importance of clear communication and the establishment of clear roles that fit skills and expectations in order to establish a collective commitment to the evaluation; and, moreover, the need to get clarification on how we could access potential sources of data.

During the evaluation planning session, the client advised us that we would be provided with contacts for previous program participants in order to gather information. This substantially facilitated the number of teacher participants who were able to provide direct feedback on their perspectives of Xplore! Also, unexpected issues arose during the evaluation, which were beyond our control, and provided an opportunity for the evaluation team to work collaboratively throughout the evaluation process.

The application of the MCE information and strategies was particularly helpful in creating a positive relationship with the CMs and other stakeholders. It also made everyone aware of each step of the collaborative evaluation beforehand to obtain the maximum benefits that can be derived from it. The MCE was a very valuable tool because it provided a logical structure and detailed methodology for the collaborative evaluation. It also helped create a sense of ownership for those at Xplore! The stakeholders most closely associated with Xplore! continued to implement this program long after the evaluation was completed.

NOTE

1. We are using a pseudonym, Xplore! Marine Life program, to protect the confidentiality of our client.

CHAPTER 4

Collaborative Evaluation of a Multisite, Multipurpose, Multiyear Early Childhood Quality Care Initiative

Rita Goldfarb O'Sullivan

As O'Sullivan (2004) notes, "Collaborative evaluation engages key program stakeholders actively in the evaluation process. Unlike distanced evaluation, where evaluators have little or no contact with program staff, collaborative evaluation deliberately seeks involvement from all program stakeholders during all stages of the evaluation" (p. 23). In support, Rodríguez-Campos (2005) wrote, "Collaborative evaluation is an evaluation in which there is a significant degree of collaboration between the evaluator and stakeholders in the evaluation process" (p. 1). Thus, a collaborative evaluation stance often leads to stakeholder involvement throughout the evaluation, a situation that must be managed. This chapter uses a multisite, multiyear evaluation of an early childhood Quality Care Initiative as an example of a collaborative evaluation.

A COLLABORATIVE EVALUATION APPROACH

A collaborative evaluation approach is one that actively engages key program stakeholders in the evaluation to the extent that they are able and willing to participate. Prior to beginning an evaluation, levels of collaboration are explored and negotiated. The negotiation could lead to high levels of involvement in the evaluation by stakeholders to virtually no involvement by stakeholders. Ideally, the negotiation process assesses stakeholder evaluation capacity (including willingness to be involved) and creates an evaluation plan that will allow for the collection of quality information to answer evaluation questions; it also hopes to enhance the evaluation expertise of participating stakeholders. This adds appreciable importance to the steps surrounding the initial clarification of an evaluation request. (See Chapters 2 and 3 for additional discussion about collaborative evaluation.)

COLLABORATIVE EVALUATION SEQUENCES

Collaborative evaluation projects follow paths equivalent to traditional evaluations and use conventional empirical research methods. Evaluation questions (hypotheses) are identified, and then data are gathered to answer the evaluation questions (to test the hypotheses). Techniques to gather data are selected from the common research toolbox of sampling and data collection strategies. Once the data are collected, they are analyzed and summarized for reporting. While these steps are very much the same as they would be for almost any other evaluation or applied social science research project, the key differences concerning collaborative evaluations are how the techniques are implemented and by whom. Furthermore, the sequencing of events and the communication around these events are extremely important and not necessarily linear.

At Evaluation, Assessment, and Policy Connections (EvAP) in the School of Education at the University of North Carolina at Chapel Hill, O'Sullivan (2014) identified a set of collaborative evaluation techniques that have worked well with multisite, multiyear evaluations. While multiple years to conduct an evaluation are not essential, they certainly do provide a stable base upon which to build relationships and enhancements in ongoing evaluation expertise. The four steps in the cycle include (1) review program status, (2) develop evaluation plans, (3) implement the evaluation, and (4) share evaluation findings (see Figure 4.1). With each of these steps recommended evaluation techniques support the collaborative process. Throughout, communication that exchanges important information and provides for flexibility between evaluator and key program stakeholders is essential. The works of O'Sullivan and Rodríguez-Campos, as outlined in a special issue of *Evaluation and Program Planning* (Vol. 35, No. 4, 2012), best represent how such evaluations are planned

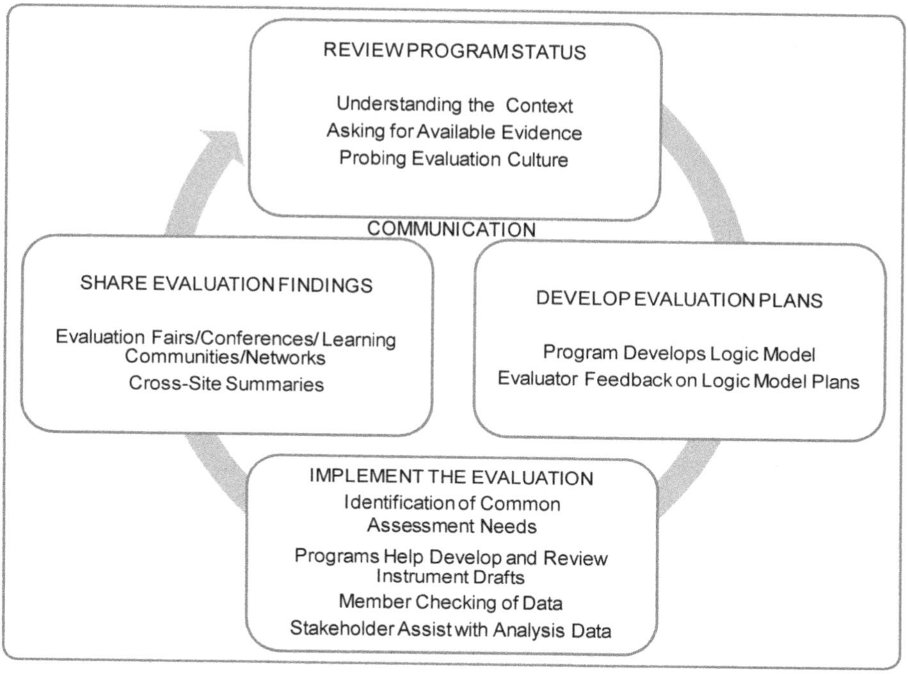

FIGURE 4.1. Four-step collaborative evaluation cycle.

and implemented. Figure 4.1 depicts the annual cycle of activities associated with such a collaborative evaluation with recommended collaborative techniques.

COLLABORATIVE EVALUATION TECHNIQUES

Review Program Status

Among things to consider at this beginning stage are *understanding the context of the program,* which would include the cultural and political contexts within which the program operates, as well as the particulars of the program content and its status vis-à-vis similar programs; *asking for any available evaluation evidence,* which would include previous evaluation and monitoring reports, proposals, and internal reports; and *probing the evaluation culture,* which would include the organization's previous experiences with evaluation, other evaluation requirements across the agency, evaluation expertise and other resources available to assist with the evaluation, and reluctance or willingness of program personnel to engage in evaluation.

Develop Evaluation Plans

Collaborative techniques start with evaluation planning, which usually begins with training around the format of the desired plan, as well as a discussion of the cross-site evaluation needs. Coupled with this discussion is an emphasis on grantees adding site-specific evaluation questions to their evaluation plans. In most cases grantees/sites are asked to *develop a logic model for their evaluation* whose format has been developed in consultation with the client organization. The *evaluator provides feedback about the grantee/site-generated logic models* and then asks grantees to work on subsequent drafts if necessary. Essential here is that the plan remain the grantee's. During this phase of the collaborative evaluation, evaluators usually find that about one-third of the grantees are able to do this activity with very little assistance beyond the initial planning meeting, another third will require two to three drafts to complete the task, and the final third may require extensive technical assistance to complete their logic models.

Implement the Evaluation

Because evaluators have already identified the cross-site evaluation requirements and seen drafts of all the logic models in the previous step, they are in a position to *identify common assessment needs across sites.* This is something that most evaluators' skill sets cover and grantees/sites appreciate, not to mention that it provides an increased potential for developing more valid and reliable instruments. As part of common instrument construction, *program staff members help develop and review instrument drafts.* This technique places more program experts around the review table to safeguard content validity, language appropriateness, and realistic data collection procedures. With qualitative data collection, evaluators practice (and sites are strongly encouraged to use) *member checking of data*, which provides opportunities for participants to comment on and amend draft data summaries originating in focus groups and interviews. This effort makes the data collection activity more transparent and once again actively engages stakeholders. Finally, *involving grantees/sites in data analysis* is a technique that strengthens the quality of information by validating interpretations about the program that can be made.

Share Evaluation Findings

The primary vehicle for this step is a networking technique, known by a variety of names: *evaluation fairs, conferences, learning communities,* and *network meetings.* With this activity grantees/sites are told at the evaluation planning stage that they will be brought together at the end of the year to share their evaluation findings. In consultation with the client organization and other key stakeholders, evaluators set the outline for the oral presentations and usually require grantees to submit a written report at the same time. The power of the event is incredible on a number of levels: providing a time for grantees/sites to celebrate accomplishments; allowing other grantees to hear about promising practices; and offering a forum that over time contributes to strengthened evaluation reporting. Evaluators then use the written reports and oral presentations to *develop cross-site summaries of accomplishments.*

This multisite, collaborative evaluation system has been used in a variety of program settings both large and small, including early childhood education, translational medicine, education, substance abuse prevention, organizational development for nonprofits, sustainable agriculture, college access, school career awareness, literacy, and K–12 international presenter programs.

POSITIVE EFFECTS OF COLLABORATIVE EVALUATION

Using a collaborative evaluation approach can result in a number of positive outcomes that both directly and indirectly affect the evaluation along with participating stakeholders and programs. Foremost is the fact that collaborative evaluation has been shown to improve data collection and reporting. Furthermore, the approach is cost-effective in that it includes program staff as part of the evaluation team, thereby reducing the number of external evaluators needed to collect data for the evaluation. The grantee/site staff and the client organization's participation in a collaborative evaluation enables them to better understand the evaluation process and thereby become better consumers of evaluation. The process also is empowering to them as they learn that they can actively manage what previously seemed daunting and unmanageable. The following section of this chapter explains how a collaborative evaluation approach was used and resulted in more useful information for stakeholders.

THE QUALITY CARE INITIATIVE EVALUATION

The Quality Care Initiative was situated within a newly formed organization, serving a very populous U.S. county. The organization had made its first program allocation of $12 million to 18 programs for a 3-year period, so that they could improve services to children under 6 years old and their families in the areas of literacy, health, quality care/training, and special needs. The following year the organization recommended a second 3-year allocation of $59.1 million, which funded an additional 35 agencies to implement programs with similar foci. None of these programs share a common program organization. All 53 programs uniquely identified which of the five foci they addressed, with some focusing only on one, while others focused on multiple areas. The organization selected the external evaluators from a competitive proposal process, in part because they thought that the collaborative evaluation approach described by the evaluators would be well suited to the organization, the variety of projects it funded, and the Quality Care grantees.

Evaluation Design

The first phase of the evaluation (Phase I) began as the first cohort of 18 grantees was already halfway through their 3-year grant, and the second cohort of 35 grantees had been in existence for 6 months. Using information gathered from grantee proposals, reports, contracts, site visit interviews, and focus groups, the evaluation team aggregated large grantee profiles into a countywide profile that reflected the types and locations of the child care services provided. A comprehensive report of the findings was submitted to the organization.

The second phase (Phase II) of the evaluation continued for 3 years and focused on four areas: process evaluation, outcome evaluation, policy issues, and capacity building. During Phase II the evaluation team continued to track the progress of program implementation for the Quality Care Initiative. In addition, this second phase of the evaluation was used to assess the impact of the initiative in addressing important policy issues. The evaluation team gathered information from the grantees through the use of a Web-based reporting system, site visit interviews, focus groups, cluster meetings, capacity-building activities, and a meta-evaluation. The evaluation team also reviewed project documents, met regularly with the organization's staff who guided the evaluation, and attended other meetings as indicated.

The original evaluation questions for Phase II activities appear in Table 4.1.

TABLE 4.1. Early Childhood Quality Care Initiative Evaluation Questions

Process evaluation

1. To what extent has the Board of Directors facilitated the work of the grantees?
2. What barriers or challenges have been encountered in the implementation of grantee programs, projects, or services?
3. How, if at all, have these implementation barriers or challenges been addressed?
4. In what ways can the client organization improve its support of grantee efforts?
5. In what ways are grantees moving toward sustainable programming?
6. To what extent are the organization's capacity-strengthening efforts effective?
7. To what extent has the evaluation of the Quality Care Initiative been effective?

Outcome evaluation

1. To what extent have grantees met their intended objectives?
2. What outcomes have grantees accomplished?
3. What is the value added of grantee programs to county child care (e.g., additional child care spaces, enhanced training)?

Policy issues

1. Which grantee-specific performance measures are most relevant to School Readiness Indicators?
2. How have local areas and county-level indicators of school readiness changed?
3. What is the link between changes in children's welfare indicators and grantee efforts?
4. What can the experiences of the grantees teach us about the county's future child care needs?

Capacity building

1. To what extent have the client organization's staff, grantees, and board members enhanced their capacity to understand and apply sound evaluation practices?
2. To what extent has the client organization expanded its utilization of evaluation findings?

Evaluation activities as they were planned and carried out appear in Table 4.2. These activities included site visits to all 53 grantees, regular meetings with the client organization's staff, and periodic meetings with consultants, the evaluation advisory committee, and the board of directors. Additionally, the evaluators worked with staff to develop a Web-based performance measurement tracking system (PMTS) to ease reporting requirements. Furthermore, evaluators conducted focus groups with grantees to collect data about process and outcome indicators. A meta-evaluation also was commissioned to provide information about the evaluation. Finally, both grantees and evaluators attended evaluation meetings to share findings and methodologies. Evaluators summarized outcome data across grantees and in the context of the identified policy indicators of school readiness.

Collaborative Elements Involving Stakeholders Initially Embedded in the Evaluation

Because the evaluation was originally designed to use a collaborative approach, it already included a great deal of stakeholder participation. The fact that the evaluation plan included a capacity-building component for board members, client organization staff, grantees, and community partners underscores the collaborative nature of the work. Thus, stakeholder participation was assumed, invited, and elicited throughout the evaluation. The sections below describe highlights of that involvement, underscoring the benefits of a collaborative stance as well as the ongoing need to be responsive to changes in client situations and needs.

Review Program Status

The first 3 months of Phase I were spent getting to know the organization and the 53 initiative grantees by reviewing the available proposals and reports as well as conducting site visits. An unusual aspect of the evaluation was that Phase I was only 6 months in length and the design of Phase II, which was planned to last 3 years, was one of the outcomes of Phase I. Given the variations in scope and breadth of the 53 projects, coupled with the newness of the organization, the 6-month design time was essential to understanding how best to design Phase II.

During this 6-month period, important foundations for future collaborative evaluation relationships were established. While project status could have been summarized almost exclusively by electronic means by

TABLE 4.2. Early Childhood Quality Care Initiative Evaluation Activities

Type of evaluation activities	Year 1	Year 2	Year 3
Process	• Grantee site visits • Grantee focus groups • Meetings with staff, consultants, evaluation advisory group, and board • Meta-evaluation	• Grantee site visits • Grantee focus groups • Meetings with staff, consultants, evaluation advisory group, and board • Meta-evaluation	• Grantee focus groups • Meetings with staff, consultants, evaluation advisory group, and board • Meta-evaluation
Outcomes	• Development and field testing of tracking system (PMTS) • Grantee focus groups • Grantee site visits • Grantee cluster meetings • Evaluation conference • Cohort 1 outcome matrix	• Tracking system (PMTS) • Grantee focus groups • Grantee site visits • Grantee cluster meetings • Evaluation conference • Grantee outcome matrix	• Cohort 2 outcome matrix • Grantee focus groups
Policy	• Identification of county/SPA indicator and subindicator impacts • Grantee cluster meetings	• Analysis of county indicator and subindicator impacts • Design and implementation of collaborative pilot studies • Grantee cluster meetings	• County/SPA indicator and subindicator impact analysis
Capacity building	• Evaluation seminars • Grantees • Organization staff • County partners • Commission • Evaluator meeting	• Evaluation seminars • Grantees • Organization staff • County partners • Commission • Evaluator meeting	• Evaluation seminars • Grantees • Organization staff • County partners • Commission
Products	• Evaluation seminars • Focus group summaries • Cohort 1 outcome matrix • Evaluation conference summary • Rubric of quality • Meta-evaluation report	• Evaluation seminars • Focus group summaries • Cohorts 1 and 2 outcome matrix • Evaluation conference summary • Pilot study findings • Meta-evaluation report	• Evaluation seminars • Focus group summaries • Cohorts 1 and 2 outcome matrix • Pilot study findings

going through all the project documents, summarizing the information on the project profiles remotely, and sending the project profiles for verification via e-mail, the evaluators purposely chose to conduct in-person site visits. The primary purpose of the site visits was to compile project snapshots (e.g., objectives, activities, size and scope of the organization), which would greatly assist with understanding the scope of the projects and future evaluation planning. A secondary purpose, and almost as important, was to introduce evaluators to the grantees, so that grantees could put a "face/person" with future interactions. To reinforce this relationship building, members of the evaluation team were assigned to specific grantees with five evaluators each responsible for 10–11 project sites.

These site visits also included a process evaluation aspect that asked grantees about their experiences with grant administration and monitoring and how, if at all, it might be improved. The in-person site visits permitted the collection of more sensitive information that probably would not have surfaced in an online survey. Trust was further established with grantees in that they were asked to review the site visit summaries prior to verifying their contents before sharing them with initiative staff. Finally, the fact that these process data were communicated to the initiative staff and acted upon with negative repercussion to individual grantees demonstrated that the evaluators were a positive presence within the initiative.

Throughout Phase I, establishing effective collaborative relationships with the organization's evaluation staff was paramount. Evaluators began this process with a 2-day meeting to share and discuss evaluation plans. Meetings varied in format; some were held with individual department directors and others were organized for all the staff in a given department. In-depth planning meetings occurred with the research and evaluation specialist responsible for coordinating Phase I. Flexibility on the part of the collaborative evaluation team encouraged flexibility on the part of the research and evaluation staff. Once firmly established these relationships could function more remotely.

Develop Evaluation Plans

The organization was slightly more than 2 years old at the start of the Phase I evaluation and had set similar but different proposal and reporting requirements for the two cohorts of grantees. Thus, evaluation planning was different for each set of grantees, with Cohort 1 not having a budget line for evaluation, whereas Cohort 2 did. As the grants were already under way, there was no opportunity to change the contractually driven agreements. In preparation for site visits evaluators were able to review evaluation plans and reports from grantees and develop a rubric to assess evaluation quality, which was then shared with the client organization's staff to assist with future evaluation planning.

As part of the evaluation capacity-building component of the evaluation, evaluators held a series of evaluation trainings for grantees' staff members, client organization staff members, and community partners. These evaluation trainings were designed expressly for grantees and their needs within the client organization's monitoring and evaluation requirements. These capacity-building efforts strengthened the collaborative aspects of the evaluation. While each grantee was responsible for its own evaluation and the external evaluation team was responsible for the cross-site evaluation, capacity-building training gave all concerned a common vocabulary and a shared understanding. Grantee evaluators were listened to and respected; the collaborative external evaluators were a known entity. As a result, grantees often used the technical assistance proffered, and data that the external evaluation team needed to collect were forthcoming. Grantees viewed the collaborative evaluation team as allies and in one case engaged their assistance in changing their external evaluator to an internal evaluator.

Implement the Evaluation

Developing the performance measure tracking system (PMTS) was one of the key process evaluation activities. When the evaluation began, grantees were required to submit written quarterly reports to the client organization with the final quarterly report inclusive of evaluation findings. For the client organization's annual reporting needs, they took each of the 53 grantees' reports and manually had to go through each one to compile the annual accomplishments. In order to move this process to a Web-based system, the evaluator brought in a Web-based data management consultant and worked with the client organization's staff to design the system they needed. This step required meetings and collaboration among the three departments in the client organization: (1) research and evaluation, (2) program development, and (3) contracts and grants, which the evaluator facilitated with the considerable assistance of the research and evaluation staff member responsible for the early childhood initiative evaluation. Beyond the client organization's staff, the grantees also needed to be consulted during the design of the PMTS. One of the evaluation meetings with grantees focused on the Web-based PMTS that was being built specifically for the initiative. At this workshop grantees received evaluation training that created a shared vocabulary around evaluation and also were able to provide essential feedback about how the PMTS should be designed and which indicators needed to be included under the various initiative outcome areas. Beyond this, grantees were recruited as volunteers to pilot-test the PMTS, which later helped during the transfer of the system to everyone.

Year 2 Focus Groups Followed by Survey

Another component of the collaborative evaluation called for annual focus groups to provide feedback to the client organization about how the organization was managing the grant process. Three focus groups were conducted with grantees. After each focus group, evaluators used member checking, sending the summary of the focus group to participants to verify its contents. Data from two of the three Year 2 focus groups yielded a number of quite negative comments that, if representative of the overall group, would be essential to share with the client organization. Attendance at these focus groups, however, only represented about one-third of the grantees, so evaluators thought that they needed to collect more data. After consultation with the client, evaluators used data from the focus groups to develop a written questionnaire, which was then completed by each of the 53 grantees. These written questionnaires ultimately provided useful data to the client about improving the grants management process.

Share Evaluation Findings

Collaborative evaluation organizes activities so that grantees have an opportunity to annually share accomplishments. Every year for 3 years, the evaluation of the early childhood Quality Care Initiative brought grantees together in this manner. For the evaluation fairs, grantees were asked to provide written reports, to prepare a 10-minute presentation of the evaluation findings, and to bring information about their program to share in a poster-type session. Client organization staff and board members also were invited to attend. To manage the process effectively, presentation groups were limited to no more than 12 grantees and organized by similarity of program activities. Grantee reports were used to complete cross-site summaries of accomplishments. Evaluation feedback from the fairs was always very positive.

Impact of Changes within the Client Organization on the Evaluation

Collaborative evaluators often need to be responsive and adjust the evaluation as changes occur within the client organization's structure and personnel. For example, at the beginning of this particular evaluation, the client organization was only 2 years old but it was growing exponentially. New initiatives were in the process of being planned and launched; new staff members were being hired; and organizational policy was being refined and/or refocused. This led to structural changes in the organization that affected the evaluation and its design.

Quarterly Reports

The organization had already gone through three different versions of the quarterly report in 2 years. Much is done in a start-up organization that requires modification based on experience; such was the case with the quarterly report. From the evaluation site visits and process evaluation focus groups, evaluators discovered that the grantees found this change process to be frustrating. Upon hearing the evaluation findings, client organization staff members were able to use this information to better communicate changes in more reasonable time periods.

Changes in Departmental Structures

At the beginning of the evaluation, evaluators worked directly with a member of the research and evaluation department staff but also made sure to coordinate with the other departments. Program monitoring was the purview of the program development department. The quarterly report design was shared between the two departments. In the second year of the evaluation, in part due to the process evaluation survey questionnaire that was described earlier, the executive director decided to introduce a separate grants management department that would directly interact with grantees, overseeing both monitoring and evaluation activities. This reorganization required personnel and job description shifts that necessitated an evaluation response. Approved activities for the evaluation had to be reviewed and approved by a new department head. Newly assigned grants management staff needed to be oriented to the evaluation and upcoming activities.

Refinements or Changes in Organizational Policy

At the beginning of the evaluation, Cohort 1 was half-way through its 3-year funding award. While no promises were made, many grantees expected that renewal funding would be considered. Six months before the end of their grants, Cohort 1 found out that there would be no renewals of their early childhood Quality Care Initiative grants. This policy stance, of course, changed the tenor of the evaluation for Cohort 1 and required the evaluators to respond to the situation by recognizing that the grantees' motivation to cooperate with evaluators had significantly diminished.

Personnel Changes

Personnel changes can have an appreciable effect on the evaluation and its conduct. Collaborative evaluators recognize that they must be responsive to these changes and adapt to the new person accordingly. Optimally, the only adjustment the evaluator needs to make is to orient the new person to the evaluation and activities planned. But occasionally personnel changes require greater responsiveness.

Within the first 6 months of the evaluation the research and evaluation staff member who was assigned to work with the initiative evaluators left to accept another position. Happily, the person assigned as a replacement came from within the client organization and knew all about the evaluation from the previous collaborative evaluation activities, and the evaluation could proceed without much delay. On the other hand, the new grants management director was hired from outside the organization and knew nothing about the ongoing evaluation. Considering that she was attempting to organize and run the newly emerging department, the evaluation initiative was not among her highest priorities. Indeed, it took a whole month to arrange a meeting with her to review the evaluation plan. It then took another month for her to move forward on the evaluation plan. Within 6 months, she resigned, and a new director of grants management was hired. In this case the change worked well for the evaluation as this director was very interested in and supportive of the evaluation.

Changes within the Grantee/Site Organizations

Collaborative evaluators also need to accommodate changes within the grantees' organizations and personnel. At least one organization changed its mission and focus during the 3-year period; and another changed its priorities due to changes in the funding streams. These types of changes require evaluators to make the effort to communicate with grantees, so that they may be apprised of events that might change evaluation efforts. Changes in personnel also occur that require retraining or additional evaluator assistance. Evaluators found during the final site visits that were conducted at the end of Year 3 with Cohort 2 grantees that many of the grantees had changed personnel; thus questions about changes in outcomes during the 3 years were virtually impossible to answer, which required heavier reliance on documentary sources than initially envisioned.

Changes in the Scope of Work

The evaluation plan is just that, and almost all good plans should be subject to change. Collaborative evaluators understand this reality. With the early childhood Quality Care Initiative, the evaluation scope of work changed in response to a variety of situations.

Expanded Evaluation Training

As a result of previous work done as part of the collaborative evaluation, including the evaluators' efforts to share evaluation methodology and findings throughout the client organization, the department director requested evaluation trainings for the newly formed grants management staff, as well as for grantees from another initiative. Collaboration here in providing the additional trainings meant that the grants management staff could share a common evaluation vocabulary and consider monitoring and evaluation for each of the initiatives from an organizational perspective. Results of the grants management evaluation training yielded a change from quarterly to semi-annual reporting across the entire client organization initiatives.

Rubric Development

Another example of how the evaluation scope of work changed in response to the client organization's needs occurred when the grants management department asked the evaluators to help them develop a rubric that would measure the quality of the semi-annual progress reports. This request was part of a no-cost extension to the evaluation contract that emerged from previous collaborative work done with the grants management department. Four of the ongoing initiatives were using similar but different templates for scopes of work, interim reports, and final reports. Evaluators reviewed the forms and developed a rubric of quality for each, which was shared first with the grants management staff. Staff members then pilot-tested the interim report rubrics with grantees. This overall responsive effort led to substantial streamlining of the reporting process.

CONCLUSION

The purpose of this chapter is to demonstrate how collaborative evaluation was used in a multisite, multipurpose, multiyear early childhood Quality Care Initiative, which resulted in useful information to stakeholders. In general, a collaborative evaluation approach involves substantial stakeholder involvement throughout the evaluation and requires adapting evaluation strategies to ever-changing stakeholder needs and situations.

For the early childhood Quality Care Initiative, the collaborative evaluation strategies used included:

- Reviewing program status, using Phase I to design Phase II of the evaluation.
- Making efforts early on to establish relationships of trust with evaluation stakeholders.
- Developing and refining evaluation plans for grantee activities that involved different outcomes.
- Providing stakeholder-specific evaluation training for grantee staff members, client organization staff members, and community partners.
- Implementing the evaluation by developing a performance measure tracking system (PMTS) with substantial assistance from client organization staff members and grantees.

- Supplementing evaluation evidence with newly proposed data collection activities to verify findings.
- Sharing evaluation findings through the use of evaluation fairs.

Communication efforts for this collaborative evaluation were highlighted by:

- Changes within the client organization's structure and personnel that required the evaluator to make contextual adjustments to the evaluation.
- Changes within the grantee organizations that required similar adjustments.
- Changes in the initial scope of work that emerged from the previous evaluation activities and findings.

A key lesson learned throughout this collaborative evaluation of the early childhood Quality Care Initiative was that communication was crucial to positive outcomes. Systematic engagement of stakeholders in the process created an environment in which people were aware not only of what was going on, but why it needed to happen. Thus, evaluators must regularly make efforts to communicate with stakeholders who may join the evaluation efforts in progress to make sure they support the plans. With such a collaborative environment, when assistance or adaptations are needed, stakeholders are more likely to cooperate; they also are more likely to use the evaluation's findings, which should result in program improvement.

CHAPTER 5

Essentials of Participatory Evaluation

Ann P. Zukoski and Cate Bosserman

Participatory evaluation is a stakeholder-driven approach in which program planners and participants actively engage with an evaluator to implement an evaluative process. This method is used widely throughout the United States and in international settings to create opportunities to engage diverse groups in evaluation (e.g., young people in the United States, social activists in Bangladesh, and indigenous communities in Columbia) (Guijt & Gaventa, 1998; Jupp, Ali, & Barahona, 2010; Sabo Flores, 2003, 2007). Participatory evaluation enhances evaluation use by increasing the depth and range of participation. It builds on participatory action research (PAR) and participatory research models. Participatory evaluation, much like other similar approaches, has benefited from ongoing critiques designed to help define it and distinguish it from other stakeholder involvement approaches (Daigneault & Jacob, 2009; Fetterman, Rodríguez-Campos, Wandersman, & O'Sullivan, 2014).

DEFINITION

Participatory evaluation is a stakeholder involvement approach to evaluation that enables evaluators and stakeholders to design and implement an evaluation together, leading to joint ownership and joint control of the evaluation process and learnings (Cousins & Whitmore, 1998). Decision making and leadership of the process begins with the evaluator and over time is divested to program stakeholders (Cousins et al., 2013; Fetterman et al., 2014). Levels of stakeholder participation vary widely from nominal to transformative, depending on the purpose of the evaluation (Cornwall, 2008; Guijt, 2014). In addition, participation can occur at any stage of the evaluation process in the design, data collection, analysis, and reporting phases (Cousins et al., 2015; Guijt, 2014; Jackson & Kassam, 1998; Shulha, 2000; Upshur & Barretto-Cortez, 1995; Zukoski & Luluquisen, 2002). According to Cousins and Earl (1992), participatory evaluation typically involves "a relatively small number of primary users" (p. 400). However, Guijt (2014) explains that involvement can include a range of different stakeholders, but the emphasis should be on "meaningful participation of programme participants" (p. 4). Participatory evaluation is designed to ensure that the evaluation addresses relevant questions that can inform program improvement (Chambers, 2009; Guijt, 2014).

TWO STREAMS

Participatory evaluation, similar to empowerment evaluation,[1] has two streams: practical and transformative. Practical participatory evaluation is pragmatic. It is focused on use, not on empowerment. It is rooted in organization learning theory and designed to support program or organizational decision making and problem solving. Transformative participatory evaluation is rooted in principles of emancipation and social justice (Cousins & Chouinard, 2012, pp. 23–25). Transformative participatory evaluation, unlike practical participatory evaluation, is designed to empower and give voice to members of the community with limited access to power or oppressed by dominating groups.

ADVANTAGES

There are many advantages associated with the use of participatory evaluation, including:

- *Identification of locally relevant questions.* Participatory approaches allow stakeholders to determine the most important evaluation questions to address, those that will most directly impact and improve the programs and systems that serve their communities.
- *Improving program performance.* Participatory evaluation supports

reflection about program progress and generates knowledge to support continual improvement. It can support corrective action and midcourse improvements during program implementation. The main goal is for findings to drive action and change.

- *Engaging stakeholders.* Participating in an evaluation from start to finish supports stakeholder ownership and commitment to accomplishing program goals and outcomes.

- *Building capacity.* Through the process, participants learn and strengthen their own evaluation skills. It can result in new knowledge and increased understanding of the program context. This can build a group's capacity to identify action steps and advocate for policy changes, as well as create systems for ongoing evaluation and improvement.

- *Developing teams and leadership opportunities.* The process of collaborative inquiry can create new opportunities for teamwork and leadership.

- *Sustaining organizational learning and growth.* Participatory evaluation nurtures a learning process that can be applied to other programs and projects. The techniques and skills acquired through the evaluative process can support organizations in their efforts to use data to improve program performance. (See Sette, 2016, for additional advantages to using this approach.)

ESSENTIAL FEATURES

Participatory evaluation is grounded in organizational learning theory and based on principles of engagement. The participatory evaluation process is implemented through a series of specific steps, and calls for a unique role for the evaluator. (A more detailed description of participatory evaluation is provided by Cousins & Chouinard, 2012; Cousins & Earl, 1992, 1995; Guijt, 2014; Guijt & Gaventa, 1998; Sette, 2016; Zukoski & Luluquisen, 2002).

CONCEPTUAL FRAMEWORK

Participatory evaluation is based in part on an organizational learning theoretical framework (Argyris & Schön, 1978). Organizational learning theory proposes that organizations improve performance by continually examining and learning from their own behavior. Organizational learning involves the integration of new ideas and constructs into existing mental maps and cognitive structures. This process of integration is a result of linkage mechanisms (Huberman, 1987; Mathisen, 1990), such as communication and collaborative group activity. According to Hedberg (1981), it "can only take place in the language of the learners, and on their terms" (p. 5).

Participatory evaluation enhances communication about relevant organizational concerns, creates an environment than enables people to think critically and creatively about how things are done, and generates new and ideally more effective ways of operating.

CONDITIONS

A number of conditions must be met to conduct a participatory evaluation effectively and authentically. Cousins and Earl (1992) include the following organizational requirements:

- Evaluation must be valued by the organization.
- Time and resources are required.
- Organizations need to be committed to organizational learning (to improve performance).
- Primary users must be motivated to participate in evaluation activities.
- Organization members are capable of learning how to conduct an evaluation (even though they typically begin with insufficient research experience).

In addition to having the time to devote to the labor-intensive participatory approach, and the resources to conduct a participatory evaluation, evaluators need to have a diverse set of skills, including:

- Training and expertise concerning technical skill.
- Ability to function as an "evaluator as teacher"; evaluators must be capable of training practice–based staff in the skills of systematic inquiry.
- Appropriate interpersonal and communication skills.
- Motivation to participate.
- Tolerance for imperfection.

These conditions and attributes increase the probability that the participatory evaluation will yield valuable information and be a productive experience for all participants.

PRINCIPLES

Although participatory evaluation principles have not been formally stated or ratified, the literature consistently cites a set of core principles that range from cultivating ownership to supporting learning, reflection, and action. These include:

- *Participant focus and ownership.* Participatory evaluation seeks to create structures and processes to engage and create ownership among all key stakeholders. The process seeks to honor the perspectives, voices, and knowledge of those most impacted, including program participants or recipients, who are often voiceless in the evaluation process (Canadian International Development Agency, 2001; Institute for Development Studies, 1998).
- *Negotiation and balance of power.* Participants commit to work together to decide on the evaluation approach. There is a balance of power among team members and the evaluator to determine each step of the evaluation process.
- *Learning.* Participants learn together about what is working about a program and what is not working, and together determine what actions are needed to improve program functioning and outcomes.
- *Flexibility.* The evaluation approach will change based on resources, needs, and skills of participants (Guijt & Gaventa, 1998).
- *Focus on action planning.* The main purpose of participatory evaluation is to identify points of action to improve program implementation.

ROLES OF THE EVALUATOR

In the participatory evaluation process the trained evaluator leads the process, but shares control with participants over time (Cousins et al., 2014). According to Cousins and Earl (1992), "In the participatory model the evaluator is the coordinator of the project with responsibility for technical support, training, and quality control, but conducting the study is a joint responsibility. . . . The evaluator's role may evolve into a posture of support and consultation as time elapses and local skills are developed and refined" (p. 400). Similar to other stakeholder involvement approaches, the evaluator serves as a facilitator, coach, negotiator, and capacity builder, ensuring that the process moves forward and comes to completion.

Participants can play a variety of roles and be engaged at different levels of decision making and involvement throughout the process (Sabo Flores, 2007). Participants may contribute to identifying relevant questions, planning the design, selecting appropriate measures and data collection methods, gathering and analyzing data, reaching consensus about findings, and disseminating results.

STEPS

There are many approaches to conducting a participatory evaluation. A five-step model is presented below (see Figure 5.1):

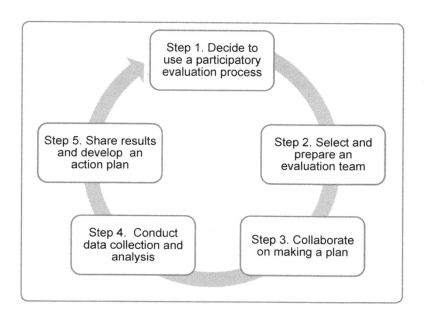

FIGURE 5.1. Participatory evaluation steps.

Step 1: Decide If a Participatory Approach Is Appropriate

Conducting participatory evaluation requires additional time, resources, and commitment to fully engage stakeholders throughout all of the steps. Considerations should include the following:

- What purpose will stakeholder participation serve to support the evaluation? Is a participatory evaluation appropriate (Guijt, 2014)?
- Are your potential team members interested? Do you have a group of people who express interest and enthusiasm?
- Does your funder support a participatory evaluation approach? Not all funders will support participatory evaluation because it may be an unfamiliar or nontraditional approach, and it may be more time- and resource-intensive than the funder desires.
- Do you have an adequate timeline? Participatory evaluation is generally a lengthier process than other evaluation approaches because it requires more time for engagement, decision making, and building consensus.
- Does your group have the potential to work well together? Does your group have the necessary skills and trust to do challenging work and resolve conflicts?

It is not necessary to have all of these factors in place to move forward. However, enthusiasm for the project among the group members, funder support, adequate time, and the potential for participants to build mutual trust are important building blocks for a successful participatory evaluation process.

Step 2: Select and Prepare an Evaluation Team

Participatory evaluation requires participation from a broad range of stakeholders. Stakeholders may include program recipients, program staff, organizational leadership, and funders. It is important to include those with different roles, knowledge, and power within the program context, including people who are most affected by a program. While asking for broad representation is a good place to start, it may be appropriate to establish a smaller working group with representatives of different stakeholder groups to enable the process to move forward in a timely manner.

All members of the evaluation team or workgroup should be oriented to align the goals of the group and ensure a shared understanding of the evaluation process. Together the group should be determined to participate in the decision-making process, and establish a mechanism for handling power differentials and potential conflicts. Groups will need to be aware of existing power dynamics, and work to actively counter them. An appreciation for the dynamics related to differences in power among those with diverse cultural, language, and socioeconomic backgrounds is imperative. The role of an evaluator is to coach the group through the formation process, and to continue to facilitate, educate, and train the group throughout the evaluation.

Establishing clear roles is critical to the participatory evaluation process. The UNICEF Methodological Brief on Participatory Approaches provides a set of questions that can guide decisions about what roles stakeholders should play in each step of the evaluation, from framing the questions to supporting use of evaluation findings (Guijt, 2014; UNICEF, 2005).

Step 3: Collaborate on Creating an Evaluation Plan

Collectively, the group with direction from the evaluator will:

- Define the evaluation priorities.
- Identify evaluation questions.
- Select indicators that the group views as important for documenting change or demonstrating evidence of progress.
- Agree on appropriate ways to collect the information, and create plans for data collection, analysis, interpretation, and the development of an action plan.

Step 4: Conduct Data Collection and Analysis

Determining a data collection methodology that builds on team strengths and maximizes team participation requires thought and consideration (Guijt & Gaventa, 1998; Zukoski & Luluquisen, 2002). Participatory evaluation can include both quantitative and qualitative approaches, and may or may not directly involve evaluation team members in data collection activities.

Rapid appraisal techniques have often been used to actively engage program participants in international settings (Chambers, 2009; UNICEF, 2005). These methods are simpler, quicker, and less costly than other data collection methods. When engaging participants in data collection, evaluators should select methods that are both rigorous and easy to use. These methods should be appealing to participants, and take relatively short amounts of time to accomplish (Canadian International Development Agency, 2001). The role of participants should be acknowledged, and participants should be compensated when appropriate.

Step 5: Action Planning

Following the gathering of data, the group should work to collectively develop a shared understanding of the evaluation results. The group should develop recommendations based on evaluation findings, and create an action plan to begin program improvement (Zukoski & Luluquisen, 2002).

CONCLUSION

Participatory evaluation represents a useful approach to engaging stakeholders in the evaluation process. This chapter focuses on critical features of participatory evaluation, including organizational learning theory, principles, roles, and steps. This brief description is designed to help practitioners distinguish one stakeholder involvement approach from another.

NOTE

1. Empowerment evaluation began with a transformative empowerment evaluation approach and evolved a second stream: practical empowerment evaluation. Participatory evaluation started with a practical participatory evaluation approach, referred to as "only participatory evaluation." It specifically stated that it was not empowering in nature (Cousins & Earl, 1995). Later the transformative participatory evaluation approach emerged.

CHAPTER 6

A Participatory Evaluation of a Community Health Improvement Initiative

Ann P. Zukoski, Cate Bosserman, and Courtney Baechler

This chapter highlights how a participatory evaluation approach engaged stakeholders to capture the impact and lessons learned from a 3-year community-based health improvement initiative. As rates of chronic disease such as heart disease and Type 2 diabetes have continued to increase across the country, communities have sought out new models for prevention. This initiative funded multisector collaboratives in 13 communities across Minnesota and western Wisconsin to create local solutions to prevent chronic disease. These community health collaboratives drew on partners, including nonprofit organizations, health systems, local businesses, and government agencies, to promote community-based prevention and wellness activities. The collaboratives achieved changes unique to each community, including strengthened relationships between the health care system and its stakeholders; sustainable policy changes in hospitals, workplaces, and schools; and environmental improvements throughout the community.

Multiple sets of stakeholders were engaged in this evaluation process from planning throughout analysis and dissemination. Central to the process was the formation of an evaluation advisory group comprised of the funder, the health system leading the implementation of the project, and the evaluation team. This chapter briefly describes the initiative, reasons for using participatory evaluation, specific steps, and concluding reflections.

THE PROGRAM/INITIATIVE

The Healthy Communities Partnership (HCP) was a 3-year program designed to improve the health of residents in 13 communities throughout Minnesota and western Wisconsin by supporting multisector health improvement initiatives. Managed by the Penny George Institute for Health and Healing, the program aimed to help prevent chronic disease and deaths related to poor nutrition, inadequate exercise, smoking, and hazardous drinking. Allina Health invested $5 million in the project through a grant to the George Family Foundation. The foundation provided administrative services to the project by managing the grant-making and evaluation functions (Allina Health, n.d.).

The HCP initiative focused on three core strategy areas: (1) enhancing and strengthening their health system's role within the local community wellness infrastructure; (2) improving community wellness through baseline biometric screening and annual re-screening activities; and (3) developing strategies to sustain community health improvement efforts through changes in organizational policies, practices, and systems and to identify resources to sustain project work. The long-term goal of this work was to improve community health outcomes.

WHY PARTICIPATORY EVALUATION?

A participatory approach allows for stakeholders to codesign the evaluation with evaluators. They share in the process of discovery as they assess a program's impact on community health. Stakeholders participate in the process of determining what evaluation questions and outcomes are most meaningful and relevant. They also participate in and support data collection and the interpretation of findings. This co-learning approach supports reflection about program progress, assessing impact, and helping the program team find new and more effective ways of operating.

The HCP evaluation advisory group was interested in closely following the development of the initiative and its outcomes, making a participatory evaluation approach an ideal fit. While cross-sector community-based approaches to chronic disease prevention are thought to be an effective strategy for improving community health, isolating and measuring the impact of these programs is complex and challenging (Zakocs & Edwards, 2006). For this reason, the evaluation team worked closely with the advisory group to identify what measures of impact would be most meaningful and feasible to collect, and to select methods that would help surface findings to contribute to this emerging approach to community-based prevention.

PARTICIPATORY EVALUATION STEPS

There are many ways to conduct a participatory evaluation. A few essential steps, discussed in Chapter 5, are applied to this evaluation. These are outlined briefly below.

Step 1: Decide If a Participatory Approach Is Appropriate

Participatory evaluation often takes more time and resources to implement when compared to other approaches. If stakeholders, such as the funder and program leaders, lack interest in participating, prefer a traditional evaluation approach, or are unfamiliar with the methods, a participatory approach may not succeed.

For this project the evaluation team proposed a participatory approach as a key component of its bid and discussed this approach at length during the selection interview. Once the evaluation team had been hired by the program funder, they took time to further explain the approach and to forecast the steps, time, and resources that would be necessary to successfully conduct an evaluation with participatory methods. Throughout the evaluation, the team found it important to revisit the strengths of conducting this approach.

Step 2: Select and Prepare an Evaluation Team

The HCP evaluation team worked closely with stakeholders at two levels. The first level included the assembly of an evaluation advisory group, comprised of key decision makers in the program. The second level involved engaging program staff and program participants in data collection, interpretation, and use of findings.

Evaluation Advisory Group

An evaluation advisory group made up of key decision makers was created to guide the work, problem-solve, and discuss emergent findings. This group included the executive director of the foundation, the foundation project manager, the medical director of the initiative, a program manager, a health system research specialist, and the external evaluation team. At the beginning of the program the advisory group met monthly; once the evaluation was launched, meetings were held quarterly throughout the 3-year project. The evaluation team worked closely with the advisory group to answer key design questions, review preliminary findings, and identify lessons learned and corrective actions. This group played an integral role in shaping and disseminating evaluation findings.

Program Staff and Participants

Program staff from all 13 grantee health systems assisted with data collection, data interpretation, and interpretation of findings. The evaluation team engaged program staff through an initial meeting to discuss the evaluation goals and methodology, and to ask for their ideas and input. The evaluation team worked closely with each grantee to implement key components of the evaluation design, and assisted grantees with the interpretation of individualized aspects of the evaluation. Evaluators shared progress updates and interim findings with grantees at biannual program meetings, and provided data in formats to promote data use by and sharing with grantees' local stakeholders.

Step 3: Collaborate on Creating an Evaluation Plan

The design and planning stages of the evaluation represent the most intense and important phase of the evaluation process. During this phase, all parties involved arrive at a shared understanding about the program, how its components fit together, and how they lead to anticipated outcomes. It is also the time to identify and prioritize evaluation questions by interest and relevance; to define clear and valid indicators; to select evaluation methods that best fit with the context in which the program is being implemented; and to envision how results will be reported and used. The evaluation team worked with the advisory group in this intensive planning process, and included grantee representatives at key points to inform the design and feasibility of the approaches.

After the initial planning phase the evaluation team invited all grantees to a World Café exercise to prioritize and surface the evaluation questions most important to them.[1] Grantees were asked to reflect on and share answers to the questions "What would success look like for you?" and "What is the most important thing you want to learn from this program?" The evaluation team also used this opportunity to explain and ask for feedback about each of the evaluation methods, including social network analysis (SNA), ripple effect mapping (REM), case studies, document review, observations, and key informant interviews.

Stakeholders' early input into the design process and ongoing feedback was invaluable for developing trust between the funder, the evaluation team, and the grantees. This relationship fostered buy-in for the evaluation, and trust in the findings that emerged. This set the foundational tone for data collection, analysis, and reporting phases.

Step 4: Conduct Data Collection and Analysis

In a participatory evaluation, stakeholders actively participate in data collection, analysis, and interpretation. Participatory evaluation designs typically rely on multiple data collection methods. For this evaluation, SNA and REM were conducted at the beginning and end of the initiative to capture change over time.

Ripple Effect Mapping

REM is used to capture program impacts at a community level, including unintended and distal impacts of a collective effort (Hansen Kollock, Flage, Chazdon, Paine, & Higgins, 2012; University of Minnesota, 2016). It involves bringing together community stakeholders with varying levels of involvement in the intervention to reflect on communitywide changes.

REM was combined with an appreciative inquiry approach in this participatory evaluation. Participants discussed and celebrated accomplishments and outcomes, creating a composite picture of how multiple efforts worked synergistically to create larger impacts within the community. Through this process, participants worked together to make meaning of these impacts by grouping effects into themes, which formed the basis for data analysis. The participatory nature of the process creates an environment conducive to capturing rich detailed stories, as well as creating new connections and energy around existing work.

The baseline REM sessions began with an appreciative inquiry interview, in which participants were asked to partner with someone whom they did not know very well, and to share a story in response to one of the following questions:

- "What is a highlight, achievement, or success you or your organization have had improving wellness through involvement with Healthy Communities Partnership?"

- "What connections with others in the community—new and/or deepened—have you made as a result of Healthy Communities Partnership?"

After a short interview process, the facilitator asked participants to report what their partner had shared. During this process a note taker began creating a map by transcribing each story onto an empty mind map template projected on a wall or screen.[2] Following the initial mapping, the facilitator posed probes encouraging participants to discuss the impacts of what they had shared, as well as downsides, limitations, or negative consequences of the project. These responses were added to the mind map, and participants were invited to begin grouping the comments into themes. Following each REM session, the evaluation team worked with the grantee project coordinator to clarify points, validate themes, and indicate which items on the map were attributable to the HCP program. After several iterations of revision and feedback, the evaluators and the project coordinator agreed on a final version of the REM, which coordinators shared with their partners.

The second round of REM sessions were conducted at the end of the grant period using the final version of the map created at that site at baseline. Each theme was isolated, enlarged, and printed on a sheet of 24″ × 36″ paper. Participants were divided into small groups consisting of four to seven participants, a facilitator, and a note taker. Groups were asked to spend 15 minutes discussing and adding to each of the themes, with the following prompts:

- "Looking at the items already on the map, have there been any developments or changes since 2013?"

- "Are there any additional health and wellness activities or changes in the community that are missing from the map?"

The group discussed their activities and used markers to edit and add to the maps. New projects and ideas were added, and projects that did not come to fruition were marked as ended. Following the sessions, the evaluation team and grantees further refined the maps in the same iterative process used at baseline, producing a final map with changes from 2013 to 2015 demarcated in different colors.

Grantees supported the REM process by (1) engaging community stakeholders, (2) hosting REM events, (3) co-facilitating group discussion, and (4) assisting with final analysis and interpretation of findings. This interaction strengthened the accuracy of the evaluation findings and provided grantees with visual, concrete examples about how the grant activities impacted their communities.

Social Network Analysis

SNA is an analysis method to explore complex relationships visually and through the use of network metrics. In an evaluation context, SNA is an effective tool for documenting changes in networks or collaborations over time. It helps to visualize, as well as quantify, the depth and breadth of relationships within or among organizations (Wendel, Prochaska, Clark, Sackett, & Perkins, 2010). A baseline analysis provides a visual mapping of the organizations involved in a collaboration, and a follow-up analysis shows the extent to which this baseline network has grown and changed over time. Fredericks and Durland (2005) identified three primary strategies using SNA: (1) examining the total structure of a network; (2) examining subnetworks formed within the total network structure; and (3) examining the connections of particular "nodes," or key players within the structure.

The HCP evaluation used this method to explore how the community collaboratives changed over the course of the grant period, and in particular how the role of local health systems changed within the collaborative. Specifically, the SNA analysis characterized collaboration among local organizations at three levels: (1) information sharing, (2) resource sharing, and (3) engagement in joint efforts.

The evaluation team used SNA as a tool to engage grantees, help them interpret their data, and use it for planning purposes. Evaluators posed questions such as "What do you see happening among your network?" and "What surprises you?" At the end of the 3-year period, grantees were asked to compare their baseline map with their final map and consider what changes occurred and why. Through these discussions, the evaluators were able to identify key reasons for structural changes in maps and included these conclusions as key evaluation findings.

Grantees assisted with the SNA work by (1) creating lists of network members; (2) informing members about the SNA survey and encouraging participation; (3) discussing their maps with evaluators; and (4) sharing the results back with their collaboratives. The interactive nature of this approach provided grantees with valuable information about their networks at the start of the evaluation so that they could plan strategically to expand or strengthen key relationships within their networks. Follow-up maps allowed grantees to gauge the success of their engagement efforts and inform plans for sustaining relationships beyond the grant period.

Step 5: Share Results and Develop an Action Plan

The evaluation team shared evaluation findings with the advisory group and with grantees at multiple points throughout the 3-year evaluation.

Advisory Group

The evaluation team supported ongoing reflection at advisory group meetings, contributing to midcourse corrections in the program. The evaluation team also introduced data to shed light on the barriers and facilitating factors that grantees experienced during their daily work. This helped the advisory group situate evaluation findings within larger contexts, including statewide and national health care and community-health contexts, and national trends in philanthropy and health funding.

Program Staff

Evaluation findings, including the community-level results of SNA and REM analyses, and thematic findings that emerged across all sites, were shared periodically with grantee program staff. Grantees used the results of their SNA to focus their efforts and seek out new community partners and measure the growth of their networks. Grantees that participated in REM used their ripple effect maps to demonstrate progress to their stakeholders, generate energy around activities, and seek out new opportunities for partnership and collaboration.

The HCP evaluation findings have been used to inform funding decisions by the family foundation who supported the effort, shape program planning by a major health system, and inform long-term planning and community engagement programs by grantee hospitals and community initiatives.

CONCLUSION

This participatory evaluation highlights how stakeholders can work with an evaluator to design and implement an evaluation, and together make meaning of the findings. In this example, multiple groups of stakeholders participated in evaluation design, data collection, analysis, interpretation, and reporting. This approach also created a positive and inclusive process for better understanding the impact of this complex program. Participatory evaluation creates a synergistic effect between the evaluation team and the core stakeholders and contributes to reflective and mutually beneficial learning.

NOTES

1. World Café is an effective method for facilitating large-group dialogue by creating small groups that rotate to multiple tables and engage in discussion of questions carefully constructed for a specific purpose. Findings are harvested and shared with the larger group (Brown, Isaacs, & the World Café Community, 2008).

2. Mind maps were created using the XMind Web application: *www.xmind.net*.

CHAPTER 7

A Participatory Evaluation of a Community Justice Program for Sex Offenders

Jill Anne Chouinard

This chapter describes a participatory approach to the evaluation of a national, community-based integration program for high-risk sex offenders conducted over a 3-year period. As the leader of a team of evaluators engaged in the evaluation of a program situated within a complex social and political ecology, it was a struggle for me to situate this social inquiry practice within a participatory methodological framework that would make sense for these stigmatized populations, and that could have the potential to make a meaningful difference in their lives and in the communities in which they live. This chapter begins with a brief definition of participatory evaluation and the rationale for its use within this specific program context, followed by a description of the program and an overview of the key phases involved in implementing a participatory process. The chapter concludes with a short description of challenges to and areas of success within the evaluation.

PARTICIPATORY EVALUATION PRINCIPLES OF PRACTICE

There are numerous types of participatory approaches to evaluation, all of which involve the inclusion of stakeholders working alongside an evaluator in the inquiry process. Among the more elaborated approaches, such as practical participatory evaluation, transformative participatory evaluation, deliberative democratic evaluation, and responsive evaluation, distinctions can be made based on the level and nature of stakeholder involvement, as well as justifications for the specific approach. Stakeholder involvement includes level of control in technical decision making, diversity among stakeholders, and depth of participation (Cousins & Whitmore, 1998).

Participatory approaches can also be distinguished based on the rationale and goals of the evaluation (political, philosophical, or pragmatic), contextual specificity, programmatic emphasis, and political orientation. In a systematic review of the literature on participatory evaluation that included the analysis of 121 studies that spanned the globe and covered a 15-year period (see Cousins & Chouinard, 2012), 56 different approaches to participatory practice were identified, including practical participatory evaluation, transformative participatory evaluation, stakeholder-based evaluation, and democratic deliberative evaluation, reflecting the cultural diversity and complexity of program and community contexts.

The use of participatory approaches is thought to provide a way to address the complexities involved in the setting (King, Nielsen, & Colby, 2004), to be more responsive to cultural context than traditional or mainstream approaches (Chouinard & Hopson, 2016), to better meet community needs and build on community strengths (Fisher & Ball, 2005), and to provide a more inclusive and empowering dynamic (Endo, Joh, & Cao Yu, 2003). From this vantage point, and within the context of the sex offender program, building a participatory context for evaluation was seen (perhaps even retrospectively) as a civic response (Spivak, 2008), as a way to open up the narrative features of evaluation practice and create a more inclusive and engaging environment across and among all stakeholder groups. The use of a participatory approach with this program is consistent with the view of evaluation as a critical social science (Fay, 1975) defined by a distinct "ethic of engagement" (Schwandt, 1997), highlighting the centrality of values (Hall, Ahn, & Greene, 2011) and advocacy (Greene, 1997). What set this evaluation apart from others in the criminal justice field was the adoption of a participatory approach, as the dominant focus in the evaluation of criminal justice programs is on the "three E's"—economy, efficiency, and effectiveness—a focus that translates into the use of "evidence-based practices" grounded principally in the use of scientific methods (Tilley & Clarke, 2006). A participatory approach thus provided an alternative perspective from an evaluation valued not for its strong internal validity and experimental rigor and expertise, but rather for its responsiveness to local and community needs, and for its commitment to diversity and engagement with a plurality of perspectives.

A DESCRIPTION OF THE PROGRAM

The reintegration program for high-risk sex offenders is a national program that provides support for and accountability to sex offenders who have been designated as at a high risk to reoffend. Many of these sexual offenders have a long history of offending, have failed in previous treatment, and have displayed intractable antisocial values and attitudes. The goal of the program is to promote successful integration of released men back into society by providing support, advocacy, and a way to be meaningfully accountable in exchange for living safely. The strength of the model is based on its volunteers, who work in small groups to provide support to ex-offenders in their transition to the community. The relationship between the ex-offenders and the volunteers is essential to the success of the program, as the support these volunteers provide stands outside of, or apart from, the formal, professionally based support system. In fact, the program is premised on the theory that assistance, support, and accountability offered in the context of friendship will lead to successful integration within the community.

This evaluation involved 13 program sites located across eight provinces in Canada. While sites have somewhat distinct policies or procedures, and articulate slightly different philosophies about the nature of their services, all share a set of basic principles and values, with the common goal of protecting the community while assisting sexual offenders in entering society.

THE PHASES OF PARTICIPATORY PRACTICE

In this section I use the phases involved in conducting a participatory evaluation to describe my 3-year participatory journey evaluating the community justice program for sex offenders. These phases (creating an evaluation advisory/steering committee, identifying the evaluation focus, negotiating stakeholder participation, evaluation planning and training, evaluation plan implementation, data analysis and interpretation) are not intended to indicate a linear process, but rather to demarcate the key distinguishing junctures of participatory practice during this particular evaluation.

Creating an Evaluation Advisory/Steering Committee

In a participatory evaluation, the creation of an evaluation advisory/ steering committee provides evaluators and involved stakeholders with the opportunity to communicate on a regular basis. As Weiss (1998) has noted, committees can also serve a methodological function by providing feedback and input on design, analysis, and technical issues, or a political function by assisting the evaluator in understanding community issues, interests, and concerns. This national evaluation had a diversity of stakeholders, with different perspectives about the program, a broad range of evaluative knowledge, and vastly different interests in the use of evaluation findings. The committee was composed of a government representative, four program site coordinators from across the country, two sex offender researchers, university personnel, and nonprofit stakeholders who were managing the evaluation contract.

While the committee was not responsible for actually implementing the evaluation project, it played an important role at the start of the evaluation in determining the focus of the evaluation, in negotiating participation, as well as in providing ongoing input and feedback on data collection, analysis, and dissemination of evaluation findings. The four site coordinators on the committee were actively involved in assisting evaluators in many aspects and phases of the evaluation, such as identifying interview participants, collecting relevant and detailed program material and information on participants, and contextualizing and understanding findings. The participatory approach was further expanded to include all site staff and other relevant stakeholders who attended national gatherings (approximately 50 people), where they were all actively involved in providing input and feedback, and essentially validating preliminary evaluation findings.

Identifying the Evaluation Focus

This phase, which lasted almost 4 months, was primarily devoted to learning as much as possible about the program, the funders, the multiple stakeholders, and the diverse program contexts, with a focus on the completion of a detailed evaluation plan defining the parameters and scope of the evaluation. As this program had so many different stakeholders and contexts of practice, this time was also used to develop a program theory with the Evaluation Advisory Committee to ensure a shared understanding of the program (e.g., output and outcomes). These meetings with the committee provided the opportunity to build commitment and support for the evaluation process and to manage expectations about the participatory process. At this stage, support is essential to ensuring the future success of the evaluation process (Cousins & Earl, 1992; Torres et al., 2000). The time was also spent meeting with and conducting informal interviews with program staff and other relevant community stakeholders to learn more about the program and its context. All program documents and literature on sex offender programs and their evaluations were collected and read during this initial phase. By the end of this phase, we had a detailed evaluation plan that all committee members could support, and that represented the different value perspectives and interests of the multiple stakeholder groups.

Negotiating Stakeholder Participation

In a participatory evaluation, active stakeholder involvement in the process is paramount, as it is considered a means to encourage empowerment, promote the use of evaluation findings, and support learning. In this evaluation, the committee was composed of a diverse group of program stakeholders who had divergent perspectives, distinct information needs, with varying levels of knowledge about research and evaluation processes and practices. As a result, their level of involvement in the process differed quite significantly, with some being deeply involved throughout the process, and with others playing a far less active role. We also included all program stakeholders from across the country on an annual basis, and made sure to time these meetings with key phases in the evaluation (e.g., data analysis, case study drafts, conclusions, and recommendations).

Given the nature of this program (a national scope with local implementation) and the vulnerability of some of the stakeholders involved (e.g., the ex-offenders), an important focus was to identify relevant stakeholders from across the country who could meaningfully contribute to the evaluation and who might also benefit themselves from their involvement. Along with committee members, we also included program participants and volunteers in site-specific case studies, which included interviews with program participants every 6 months for the duration of the evaluation, and weekly journal entries from volunteers (detailing their activities with participants and progress over time). While initially program participants (ex-offenders) told us that they were willing to be involved in the evaluation simply as a way to show their gratitude to program coordinators and volunteers, after our initial meeting with them they looked forward to our interactions and seemed genuinely to open up more and more as our relationship with them developed.

Evaluation Planning and Training

In this phase of the evaluation, we worked with committee members to build a common understanding about participatory evaluation, develop consensus about the evaluation plan, clarify roles, establish timelines, identify case study sites and select ex-offenders, and prepare data collection instruments. Decisions about method selection were based on a consideration of evaluation purpose; stakeholder interests, experiences, and strengths; funder requirements; and program site contexts. Meetings were held (either virtually or in person) with committee members and, early on in the process, meetings were held with all local site staff (approximately 26 people) and other relevant program and community stakeholders to discuss the evaluation process and plan. This "gathering" of program stakeholders occurred on an annual basis, and so we used the time to engage stakeholders, build evaluation capacity, and encourage their active participation in data analysis. This inclusive, active, and engaged process helped build relationships with stakeholders from across the country as well as overall buy-in for the evaluation. It also enabled us to adapt our evaluative practice to local conditions and accommodate the diverse needs of the stakeholder population. This adaptation involved developing skills that included mediation, facilitation, coaching, organizational development, conflict management, extending far beyond the scope of traditional evaluation training (Mercier, 1997). Moreover, because this evaluation extended over a 3-year period, we were able to build on previous training, follow up with local stakeholder groups, and monitor their learning and development needs throughout the duration of the evaluation.

Evaluation Plan Implementation

While this is an ongoing process throughout the evaluation, it is worth noting that at the outset it requires negotiating entry into the community and gaining access to program sites and to the people who possess relevant program and community knowledge. Working with local program coordinators (and in some cases with volunteers) is essential, as it helps with navigating entry into these communities of practice.

In a participatory evaluation, the data collection processes tend to emerge out of the local context, community, and program circumstances. Despite an earlier evaluability assessment of the program with findings suggesting that the program was not ready for an impact evaluation, and despite ongoing efforts to reframe the evaluation to focus on criteria outside of recidivism rates (e.g., the perspectives and experiences of "other" stakeholders), the emphasis on the use of experimental methods endured throughout the almost 3 years of work on the evaluation. As such, it became necessary to move continuously between the personal biographies (and narratives) of the stakeholders and the persistent need to fulfill the requirements of the evaluation. As Kushner (2000) has noted in a more challenging evaluation experience, it becomes difficult to find the right language to weave together all the different threads of the initiative, to find some coherence among what are so often discordant personal, political, and methodological narratives.

Data Analysis and Interpretation

In a participatory evaluation, it is often productive to involve stakeholders directly in the analysis, interpretation of findings, and development of conclusions and recommendations. Over the course of this evaluation, the committee met regularly to discuss findings and create shared meanings about what the findings might indicate. Findings were also shared with a wider stakeholder group at annual gatherings, where whole-group meetings were facilitated to help with data analysis and interpretation. After one of the first annual meetings, when an entire day was spent discussing findings, a junior evaluator observed that the meeting had been a "total failure" because the stakeholders were not knowledgeable enough about evaluation to help us in our work. My response was that we had just spent a whole day with all program stakeholders discussing evaluation, a rare occurrence in our kind of work, and a fine example of "process use" in participatory practice. This process of dialogue in the co-construction of knowledge among such a large and diverse group of stakeholders highlights the fundamentally relational, interactive, and learning features of the participatory approach, with consequences that include capacity building, team building, increased ownership, and empowerment.

CONCLUSION

Working in a context where program participants are among the most demonized in our society requires an explicit and vocal engagement with values, in terms of the decisions that we make about inclusion and our sociopolitical responsiveness to the program and community context. A participatory approach to the evaluation of this program enabled actively engaging with a diverse group of stakeholders throughout the process, building relationships with communities, and developing a far greater understanding of the program and program participant experiences. One of the key benefits of the approach is in the learning that takes place both at a practical level in terms of the program and community context, and at the conceptual level concerning relationships to self and to others. As a fundamentally relational and pedagogical undertaking (Schwandt, 2003), the evaluative process led to instances of "process use" (Patton, 1997b), as the participatory process enhanced reflection, learning, and changes in relationships among all stakeholders involved in the process.

While the participatory approach ensured a continuous focus on learning throughout the evaluation, the diversity of the committee (and of the stakeholders involved) also surfaced differences among stakeholders, highlighting acute disparities of power and position within and between stakeholder groups. Inequalities among stakeholders (within the broader group and among committee members) made it a challenge to ensure equitable participation, as those stakeholders unused to having a voice were afraid to speak up in the presence of more powerful stakeholders. During the course of the evaluation, because offenders were afraid to share their thoughts in whole-group settings, there were many instances where one-on-one meetings with individual committee members had to be scheduled. In my role as lead evaluator, the multiple roles of trainer, facilitator, negotiator, and mediator changed throughout the process to accommodate the exigencies, the complexity, and the context, and to help navigate differences of power and privilege among stakeholders. These multiple roles required incredible flexibility, as the struggle to accommodate the exigencies and complexity of the evaluation and program context persisted throughout. In the end, the real challenge is that if evaluation is ultimately to be of value and also to be compassionate to those who are most marginalized in our society, evaluators need to create a meaningful methodological context for *all* program stakeholders.

CHAPTER 8

Essentials of Empowerment Evaluation

David M. Fetterman and Abraham Wandersman

Empowerment evaluation is practiced throughout the United States and in over 16 countries, ranging from Australia to Israel and Japan to South Africa. It has been applied to a wide variety of settings, including Google (Fetterman & Ravitz, 2017; Ravitz & Fetterman, 2016), Hewlett-Packard's $15 Million Digital Village Initiative bridging the divide between communities of color (Fetterman, 2013b), Stanford University School of Medicine's accreditation efforts (Fetterman, 2009; Fetterman et al., 2010), Arkansas' tobacco prevention programs (Fetterman, Delaney, Triana-Tremain, & Evans-Lee, 2015), economic revitalization on Native American reservations (Fetterman, 2013b), the NASA/Jet Propulsion Laboratory's prototype Mars Rover education programs (Fetterman & Bowman, 2002), and health-related initiatives in townships and squatter settlements in South Africa.

Empowerment evaluation has also been used by educators to improve schools in academic distress in rural Arkansas (Fetterman, 2005a) and teachers evaluating their own impact within the internationally practiced Visible Learning model (Clinton & Hattie, 2015). Peruvian women have used empowerment evaluation to build small businesses and become more economically self-sufficient (Sastre-Merino, Vidueira, & Diaz-Puente, 2015). Fourth- and fifth-grade students have used empowerment evaluation to make their school more inclusive and inviting (Langhout & Fernandez, 2015). Empowerment evaluation has also been used in teen pregnancy prevention and substance abuse prevention programs (Wandersman, 2015).

The approach celebrated its 21st anniversary with a panel of luminaries at the AEA (e.g., Marvin Alkin, 2017; Stewart Donaldson, 2017; Michael Patton, 2017; and Michael Scriven, 2017). They presented both compliments and critiques. The most common observation concerned the empowerment evaluators' ability to listen, engage in discourse, and improve practice. For example:

- While I considered the exchanges invigorating and overflowing with evaluation wisdom, my most remarkable memory of the occasion was how David Fetterman modeled empowerment evaluation's characteristic orientation to openly and honestly engage in self-reflection and critique throughout the debate (see Donaldson, Patton, Fetterman, & Scriven, 2010). Fetterman and his colleagues have used this critical feedback to refine and improve their conceptual clarity and methodological specificity (Donaldson, 2017; Fetterman & Wandersman, 2007).

- I've had the privilege over the years of engaging in dialogue with David Fetterman and Abraham Wandersman and others about various aspects of empowerment evaluation. Certainly, one of the ways in which empowerment evaluation is exemplary is in its openness to dialogue and reflective practice (Fetterman, 2005b; Fetterman & Wandersman, 2007; Patton, 2005, 2015).

- A powerful, and possibly unique, application of meta-evaluation that is both ethical and pragmatic in nature. I try to match David Fetterman on this viewpoint, and indeed advocate by going further than his enthusiasms for the use of the "critical friend" to the use of the "critical enemy," but I am less successful with this second gambit. However, I never think of empirical evaluation without reflecting on his inspirational example of treating his critics as friends—and not just friends but *helpers*—as they indeed are. The connection between us is close because we are both part of that small group who *really* believes that proposition and act on it (Scriven, 2017).

Empowerment evaluation's development and refinement has greatly benefitted from decades of discourse (Alkin, 2017; Cousins, 2005; Datta, 2016; Fetterman, 1997, 2005b; Fetterman & Wandersman, 2007; Fetterman, Wandersman, & Kaftarian, 2015a; Miller & Campbell, 2006; Patton, 1997a, 2015; Scriven, 2005a; Wandersman & Snell-Johns, 2005).

DEFINITION

Empowerment evaluation is the use of evaluation concepts, techniques, and findings to foster improvement and self-determination (Fetterman, 1994). They are conducted by community and program staff members, with the assistance of a professional evaluator. It is an approach that "aims to increase the likelihood that programs will achieve results by increasing the capacity of program stakeholders to plan, implement, and evaluate their own programs" (Wandersman & Snell-Johns, 2005, p. 28). Empowerment evaluation can be conducted everywhere from small groups to large-scale comprehensive (place-based) community change initiatives. It is mainstreamed as part of the planning and management of the program/organization. In essence, empowerment evaluation is a tool to help people produce desired outcomes and reach their goals.

TWO STREAMS

Empowerment evaluation in practice is typically applied along two streams. The first is practical and the second transformative. Practical empowerment evaluation is similar to formative evaluation. It is designed to enhance program performance and productivity. It is still controlled by program staff, participants, and community members. However, the focus is on practical problem solving, as well as on programmatic improvements and outcomes.

   Transformative empowerment evaluation (Fetterman, 2015) highlights the psychological, social, and political powers of liberation. People learn how to take greater control of their own lives and the resources around them. The focus in transformative empowerment evaluation is on liberation from predetermined, conventional roles and organizational structures or "ways of doing things." In addition, empowerment is a more explicit and apparent goal.

ADVANTAGES

There are a number of advantages to using empowerment evaluation. Community and staff members are engaged and build evaluation capacity. They also learn to think evaluatively. In addition, they become more self-determined and produce sustainable outcomes. Further advantages include community and staff members:

- Producing better quality data collection, analysis, and reporting (relevant and locally meaningful)
- Using evaluation findings and recommendations (knowledge utilization as a function of ownership)
- Assuming programmatic and evaluative leadership roles and responsibilities, often otherwise denied them in society
- Addressing social justice issues

ESSENTIAL FEATURES

Empowerment evaluation's essential features include a conceptual framework guided by empowerment and process use theory, as well as by theories of use and action. Additional features include the role of the critical friend, the 10 principles, and specific steps (three-step and 10-step approaches). When combined, these features provide an insight into the dynamic and synergistic nature of empowerment evaluation. (A more detailed description of empowerment evaluation is provided in Fetterman, Kaftarian, & Wandersman, 2015.)

CONCEPTUAL FRAMEWORK

Empowerment theory is about gaining control, obtaining resources, and understanding one's social environment. Empowerment theory processes contribute to specific outcomes. Linking the processes to outcomes helps draw metalevel causal relationships or at least a chain of reasoning. This enables community members to determine the logic behind their actions.

Process use represents much of the rationale or logic underlying empowerment evaluation in practice, because it cultivates ownership by placing the approach in community and staff members' hands. The more that people are engaged in conducting their own evaluations, the more likely they are to believe in them, because the evaluation findings are their own. This makes them more likely to make decisions and take actions based on their evaluation data. This way of thinking is at the heart of process use.[1]

A by-product of conducting an empowerment evaluation is that people learn to think evaluatively. Thinking evaluatively is a product of guided immersion. This process occurs when people conduct their own evaluation with the assistance of an empowerment evaluator. Teaching people to think evaluatively is like teaching them to fish. The skill can last a lifetime and is what evaluative sustainability is all about—internalizing evaluation (individually and institutionally).

Once the groundwork is laid with empowerment and process use theories, conceptual mechanisms become more meaningful. Theories that enable comparisons between use and action are essential. For example, a *theory of action* is usually the espoused operating theory about how a program or organization works. It is a useful tool, generally based on program personnel views. The theory of action is often compared with the theory of use. *Theory of use* is the actual program reality, the observable behavior of stakeholders (see Argyris & Schön, 1978; Patton, 1997b). People engaged in empowerment evaluations create a theory of action at one stage and test it against the existing theory of use during a later stage. It helps people determine consistencies and inconsistencies in organizational and community behavior. A group can identify where and when it is not "walking its talk." This dialectic in which theories of action and use are routinely juxtaposed in daily practice creates a culture of learning and evaluation.

PRINCIPLES

Empowerment evaluation principles provide a sense of direction and purposefulness throughout an evaluation. Empowerment evaluation is guided by 10 specific principles (Fetterman & Wandersman, 2005, pp. 1–2, 27–41, 42–72):

1. *Improvement.* Empowerment evaluation is designed to help people improve program performance; it is designed to help people build on their successes and reevaluate areas meriting further attention.

2. *Community ownership.* Empowerment evaluation values and facilitates community control; use and sustainability are dependent on a sense of ownership.

3. *Inclusion.* Empowerment evaluation invites involvement,

participation, and diversity; contributions come from all levels and walks of life.

4. *Democratic participation.* Participation and decision making should be open and fair.

5. *Social justice.* Evaluation can and should be used to address social inequities in society.

6. *Community knowledge.* Empowerment evaluation respects and values community knowledge.

7. *Evidence-based strategies.* Empowerment evaluation respects and uses the knowledge base of scholars (in conjunction with community knowledge).

8. *Capacity building.* Empowerment evaluation is designed to enhance stakeholders' ability to conduct evaluation and to improve program planning and implementation.

9. *Organizational learning.* Data should be used to evaluate new practices, inform decision making, and implement program practices; empowerment evaluation is used to help organizations learn from their experience (building on successes, learning from mistakes, and making midcourse corrections).

10. *Accountability.* Empowerment evaluation is focused on outcomes and accountability; empowerment evaluations function within the context of existing policies, standards, and measures of accountability and asks "Did the program or initiative accomplish its objectives?"

Empowerment evaluation principles help evaluators and community members to make decisions that are in alignment with the larger purpose or empowerment evaluation goals associated with capacity building and self-determination.

ROLE OF THE EVALUATOR

A *critical friend* is one of the most important roles played in an empowerment evaluation (see Fetterman et al., 2010).[2] A critical friend is an evaluator who facilitates the process and steps of empowerment evaluation.[3] The friend believes in the purpose of the program, but provides constructive feedback designed to promote its improvement. A critical friend helps to raise many difficult questions and, as appropriate, tells the hard truths in a diplomatic fashion. He or she helps to ensure that the evaluation remains organized, rigorous, and honest.

The role of the critical friend merits special attention because it is like a fulcrum in terms of fundamental relationships. Applied improperly, it can be like a wedge inhibiting movement and change; applied correctly, it can be used to leverage and maximize the potential of a group. The empowerment evaluator can differ from many traditional evaluators. Instead of being the "expert" and completely independent, separate, and detached from the people with whom he or she works, so as not to become "contaminated" or "biased," the empowerment evaluator works closely with and alongside program staff members and participants. Empowerment evaluators are not in charge themselves—the people they work with are truly in charge of the direction and execution of the evaluation. Empowerment evaluators are critical friends or coaches. They believe in the merits of a particular type of program but they are willing to pose the difficult questions. Some people ask how can an empowerment evaluator be objective and critical if he or she is friends with participants and in favor of a type of program? The answer is simple: an empowerment evaluator is critical and objective *because* he or she wants the program to work (or to work better). He or she may be in favor of a general type of program, but does not necessarily assume a position about a specific program without data.

Empowerment evaluators are trained evaluators with considerable expertise. They provide it as needed to keep the evaluation systematic, rigorous, and on track. They are able to function in this capacity by advising, rather than by directing or controlling, an evaluation. They provide a structure or set of steps to conduct an evaluation. They recommend, rather than require, specific activities and tools. They listen and rely on the group's knowledge and understanding of their local situation. The critical friend is much like a financial advisor or personal health trainer. Instead of judging and making pronouncements about successes or failure, compliance or noncompliance, the empowerment evaluator serves the group or community in an attempt to help them maximize their potential and unleash their creative and productive energy for a common good. Important attributes of a critical friend include (1) creating an environment conducive to dialogue and discussion; (2) providing or requesting data to inform decision making; (3) facilitating rather than leading; (4) being open to ideas and inclusive; and (5) willing to learn (see Fetterman, 2009; Fetterman et al., 2010).

Empowerment evaluators help promote a culture of evidence by asking people why they believe what they believe. They are asked for evidence or documentation at every stage, so that it becomes normal and expected to have data to support one's opinions and views.

STEPS

There are many ways in which to implement an empowerment evaluation. In fact, empowerment evaluation has accumulated a warehouse of useful tools. The three-step (Fetterman, 2015) and 10-step Getting-To-Outcomes (Chinman, Imm, & Wandersman, 2004) approaches to empowerment evaluation are the most popular tools in the collection.

Three-Step Approach

The three-step approach includes helping a group to (1) establish their mission, (2) take stock of their current status, and (3) plan for the future. The popularity of this particular approach is in part a result of its simplicity, effectiveness, and transparency.

Mission

The group comes to a consensus concerning their mission or values (see Figure 8.1). This gives them a shared vision of what's important to them and where they want to go. The empowerment evaluator facilitates this process by asking participants to generate statements that reflect their

1. Democratic

2. Transparent

3. Group values

4. Honor existing mission but go where the energy is in the room

5. Giving voice and making meaning

FIGURE 8.1. Mission.

mission. These phrases are recorded on a poster sheet of paper (and may be projected using an LCD projector depending on the technology available). These phrases are used to draft a mission statement (crafted by a member of the group and the empowerment evaluator). The draft is circulated among the group. They are asked to "approve" it and/or suggest specific changes in wording as needed. A consensus about the mission statement helps the group think clearly about their self-assessment and plans for the future. It anchors the group in common values.

Taking Stock

After coming to a consensus about the mission, the group evaluates their efforts (within the context of a set of shared values). First, the empowerment evaluator helps members of the group generate a list of the most important activities required to accomplish organizational or programmatic goals. The empowerment evaluator gives each participant five dot stickers, and asks the participants to place them by the activities they think are the most important to accomplish programmatic and organizational goals (and thus the most important to evaluate as a group from that point on). Their use of the dots can range from putting one sticker on five different activities to putting all five on one activity if they are concerned that activity will not get enough votes. The top 10 items with the most dots represent the results of the prioritization part of taking stock (see Figure 8.2). The 10 activities represent the heart of part two of taking stock: rating (see Figure 8.3).

The empowerment evaluator asks participants in the group to rate how well they are doing concerning each of the activities selected, using a 1 (low) to 10 (high) scale. The columns are averaged horizontally and vertically. Vertically, the group can see who is typically optimistic and/ or pessimistic. This helps the group calibrate or evaluate the ratings and opinions of each individual member. It helps the group establish norms. Horizontally, the averages provide the group with a consolidated view of how well (or poorly) things are going. The empowerment evaluator facilitates a discussion and dialogue about the ratings, asking participants why they gave a certain activity a 3 or a 7, for example.

DIALOGUE

The dialogue about the ratings is one of the most important parts of the process. In addition to clarifying issues, evidence is used to support

- List activities
- Prioritize (dots)

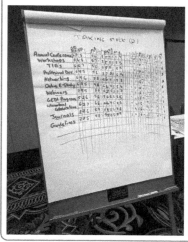

Activities	Prioritization with Dots
Communication	○○○○
Teaching	○○○○○○○
Funding	○○○

FIGURE 8.2. Taking stock: Part I.

- Rating 1 (low) – 10 (high)
- Dialogue

Activities	DF	DE	SEC	AVG.
Communication	3	6	3	4
Teaching	4	5	9	6
Funding	5	2	1	2.67
Prod Dev Develop	1	8	4	4.33
Average	3.25	5.25	4.25	(4.25)

FIGURE 8.3. Taking stock: Part II.

viewpoints and "sacred cows" are surfaced and examined during dialogue. Moreover, the process of specifying the reason or evidence for a rating provides the group with a more efficient and focused manner of identifying what needs to be done next, during the planning for the future step of the process. Instead of generating an unwieldy list of strategies and solutions that may or may not be relevant to the issues at hand, the group can focus its energies on the specific concerns and reasons for a low rating that were raised in the dialogue or exchange.

Planning for the Future

Too many evaluations conclude at the taking-stock phase. However, taking stock is a baseline and a launching-off point for the rest of the empowerment evaluation. After rating and discussing programmatic activities, it is important to do something about the findings. It is time to plan for the future (see Figure 8.4). This step involves generating goals, strategies, and credible evidence (to determine if the strategies are being implemented and if they are effective). The goals are directly related to the activities selected in the taking-stock step. For example, if communication was selected, rated, and discussed, then communication (or improving communication) should be one of the goals. The strategies emerge from the taking-stock discussion, as well, as noted earlier. For example, if communication received a low rating and one of the reasons for this was because the group never had agendas for their meetings, then preparing agendas might become a recommended strategy in the planning for the future exercise.

MONITORING THE STRATEGIES

Many programs, projects, and evaluations fail at this stage for lack of individual and group accountability. Individuals who spoke eloquently and/or emotionally about a certain topic should be asked to volunteer to

- Goals
- Strategies
- Evidence

FIGURE 8.4. Planning for the future.

lead specific task forces to respond to identified problems or concerns. They do not have to complete the task by themselves. However, they are responsible for taking the lead in a circumscribed area (a specific goal) and reporting the status of the effort periodically at ongoing management meetings. Similarly, the group should make a commitment to reviewing the status of these new strategies as a group (and be willing to make midcourse corrections if they are not working). Conventional and innovative evaluation tools are used to monitor the strategies. An evaluation dashboard is a particularly useful tool to monitor change or progress over time (see Figure 8.5). It consists of baselines, benchmarks or milestones, and goals. For example, a minority tobacco prevention program empowerment evaluation in Arkansas has established:

1. Baselines (the number of people using tobacco in their community)

2. Goals (the number of people they plan to help stop using tobacco by the end of the year)

3. Benchmarks or milestones (the number of people they expect to help stop using tobacco each month or quarter)

4. Actual performance (the actual number of people they help to stop smoking at each interval throughout the year)

Family Youth Enrichment Network

Document Support for Tobacco-Free Policies

	1st Qtr	2nd Qtr	3rd Qtr	4th Qtr
Actual performance	25	158	275 ←	
Benchmark	25	50	75	100
Goal	100	100	100	100
Baseline	0	0	0	0

Exceeded Annual Goals

FIGURE 8.5. Evaluation dashboard comparing baselines with benchmarks or milestones and goals.

These metrics are used to help a community monitor program implementation efforts and enable program staff and community members to make midcourse corrections and to replace ineffective strategies with potentially more effective ones as needed. These data are also invaluable when the group conducts a second taking-stock exercise (3–6 months later) to determine if they are making progress toward their desired goals and objectives. Additional metrics enable community members to compare, for example, their baseline assessments with their benchmarks/milestones or expected points of progress, as well as their goals.

The 10-Step Getting To Outcomes Approach

In addition to a three-step approach, there is a 10-step approach to empowerment evaluation. The 10-step approach is called Getting To Outcomes (GTO; Chinman et al., 2004). GTO is a method for planning, implementing, and evaluating programs in order to achieve success. GTO provides a framework of 10 accountability questions. When answered with quality, they provide a pathway to help programs achieve results and demonstrate accountability (see Table 8.1).

The first step is to conduct a needs and resource assessment to determine what the important issues are in the community, school, or agency. This involves collecting both qualitative and quantitative data about the problem (e.g., by using community forums, interviews, surveys, and archival documentation). The orienting question is "What are the needs and resources in your organization/community/state?"

The second step is to identify the goals, population, and desired outcomes. Set up short- and long-term (realistic) objectives to help assess progress toward desired objectives. An orienting question is "What are the goals, target population, and desired outcomes (objectives) for your organization/community/state?"

The third step is to review the literature and similar programs concerning best practices. It is not necessary to reinvent the wheel. Programs should be selected that have an established evidence base. An orienting question is "How does the intervention incorporate knowledge or science and best practices in this area?"

The fourth step is to determine how well the program or initiative (selected in Step 3) fits the needs of the population and community. This is an important stage in which to consult with community leaders about the value of the proposed program. An orienting question is "How does the intervention fit with other programs already being offered?"

The fifth step is to determine if your organization has the capacity to implement the selected program with quality. This includes funding, staffing, expertise, and community contacts. This fifth step will help to prevent program failure. One of the orienting questions is "What capacities do you need to put this intervention into place with quality?"

The sixth step is make a plan to implement your program. This includes determining (1) who will implement the program; (2) what needs to be done; (3) when, where, how, and why the tasks will be completed; and (4) what and how much will happen as a result of community participation in the program. An orientation question is "How will this intervention be carried out?"

The seventh step is to ask if the program is being implemented faithfully and with quality (at least in spirit). Describe what was done, how program activities were executed, who was served, and the detours required along the way. An orientation question is "How will the quality of implementation be assessed?"

The eighth step is to think about how you will measure whether the program has met its goals and produced desired outcomes. This involves selecting or designing an appropriate evaluation design, data collection tools, and data analysis plans. An orienting question is "How well did the intervention work?"

The ninth step is to plan for continuous quality improvement. Use existing evaluation findings to inform ongoing decision making about program operations. Develop a culture of organizational learning. An orienting question is "How will continuous quality improvement strategies be incorporated?"

Finally, the tenth step is to review sustainability considerations. Does the problem continue to exist? Does the data merit future funding? If so, identify program advocates and search for continued funding streams. An orienting question is "If the intervention is (or components are) successful, how will the intervention be sustained?"

The 10 steps are listed in Table 8.1 with their corresponding evaluation question.

These steps and guiding questions are designed to build evaluation capacity and improve the probability of program success and sustainability. There are many GTO manuals with worksheets designed to address how to answer each of the 10 questions (e.g., Chinman et al., 2004). GTO has been used in multiple domains, including substance abuse prevention, underage drinking (Imm et al., 2006), promoting positive youth

TABLE 8.1. GTO Accountability Questions

Step	Evaluation question
1. Needs assessment	"What are the needs and resources in your organization/school/community/state?"
2. Goal setting	"What are the goals, target population, and desired outcomes (objectives) for your school/community/state?"
3. Science and best practices	"How does the intervention incorporate knowledge or science and best practices in this area?"
4. Fit; cultural context	"How does the intervention fit with other programs already being offered?"
5. Capacity	"What capacities do you need to put this intervention into place with quality?"
6. Planning	"How will this intervention be carried out?"
7. Implementation/process evaluation	"How will the quality of implementation be assessed?"
8. Outcome and impact evaluation	"How well did the intervention work?"
9. Total quality management; continuous quality improvement	"How will continuous quality improvement strategies be incorporated?"
10. Sustainability and institutionalization	"If the intervention is (or components are) successful, how will the intervention be sustained?"

development (Fischer, Imm, Chinman, & Wandersman, 2006), home visiting programs (Mattox, Hunter, Kilburn, & Wiseman, 2013), and teenage pregnancy programs (Chinman, Acosta, Ebener, Sigel, & Keith, 2016).

In addition, empowerment evaluations are using many other tools, including photo journaling, online surveys, virtual conferencing formats, blogs, shared Web documents and sites, infographics and data visualization (Fetterman, 2013c), and creative youth self-assessments (Sabo Flores, 2007).

CONCLUSION

This chapter highlights critical features of empowerment evaluation. Empowerment evaluation's essential features include a conceptual framework consisting in part of empowerment theory, the theory of process use, and theories of use and action. In addition, it includes the role of the critical friend, 10 principles, and specific steps (three- and 10-step models). Together they provide guidance for practitioners in the field and help people to help themselves.

NOTES

1. There is a substantial literature concerning the use of evaluation. However, most of it is devoted to lessons learned *after* the evaluation. The discussion of process use in this context focuses on use *during* an evaluation.

2. These concepts are influenced by traditional organizational development and transformation theorists including Argyris and Schön (1978) and Senge (1994), as well as by evaluators associated with organizational learning (Preskill & Torres, 1999).

3. See Fetterman (2009) and Fetterman et al. (2010) for additional description of a critical friend.

CHAPTER 9

An Empowerment Evaluation of a Comprehensive Sex Education Initiative

Margret Dugan

Over time, those involved in an empowerment evaluation learn to appreciate the reality that knowledge comes in many forms, including data, experience, history, local wisdom, and perception. In addition, empowerment evaluators recognize that there are different perspectives on truth and real differences in power and access to knowledge. The evaluator's aim, however, remains the same: to help communities help themselves and advance science in the process.

This chapter provides an overview of core values, key themes, and pathways for action in pursuit of an empowerment evaluation of a comprehensive sex education initiative. Although this is neither a guide nor a "how-to" chapter, it nevertheless provides an introduction for individuals seeking educational content about empowerment evaluation methodology. It may also be useful for those wanting to expand existing approaches using empowerment evaluation–based practices.

THE EVALUATION CONTEXT

On March 23, 2010, President Barack Obama signed into law the Patient Protection and Affordable Care Act. The act amended Title V of the Social Security Act to include the Personal Responsibility Education

Program (PREP). The Administration on Children, Youth and Families and Youth Services Bureau (FYSB) jointly supervised the project.

The purpose of the federally funded and supported PREP is to help and assist selected states and their communities to provide evidence-based educational programs that have been proven by scientific research to change youth's sexual behavior. The principal desired outcomes of PREP are to delay the onset of sexual activity, to increase condom or contraceptive use for sexually active youth, and to reduce unplanned pregnancy and HIV/AIDS/STI transmission rates among youth ages 10–20.

Our firm, Primetime Research and Evaluation, received a contract from the State of Colorado to provide technical assistance and evaluation to ensure that the mission and goals of this project were met with fidelity, integrity, relevance, and sustainability. Our evaluation process is not linear, but it is staged. In a classic study, Rogers (1969) illustrated that when an adult learner has control over the nature, timing, and direction of the learning process, the entire experience is facilitated. With this in mind, we developed a staged system to build evaluation competence (see Table 9.1). A client may be in any stage, but each stage must be understood.

Despite this nonlinear path, the basic structure of the evaluation included a logical flow, specifically mission development, self-assessment ratings, a theory of change, a logic model, and a focus on outcomes or results. Community input, feedback, and control characterized the collection, analysis, and review of data from the beginning of stage one of the evaluation. They also helped make midcourse corrections based on the interim findings. Clients then implemented program practices based on the evaluation findings, becoming increasingly self-sufficient and self-efficacious throughout the evaluation. The following discussion highlights a continuous commitment to learning and improvement at various stages of an empowerment evaluation process.

EMPOWERMENT EVALUATION

Based on Bandura's (1977) self-efficacy theory of unifying behaviors, we define empowerment[1] as, quite simply, any process by which individuals gain mastery or control over their own lives as well as an increased ability to play an assertive role in managing resources and decisions on their own. Per Fetterman (1994, p. 2), "Empowerment evaluation is the use of

TABLE 9.1. Stages Building Evaluation Competence

Stage	Client role	Evaluator role
Stage 1: Organizing for action Evaluators provide orientation to evaluation process; demystify evaluation; build trust and confidence.	• Orient to evaluation process. • Clarify roles, policies, and procedures. • Assess program needs; identify gaps. • Gather community input/feedback. • Complete individual evaluation plan and timelines with evaluator coaching.	• Demystify evaluation process, build trust. • Acknowledge fears, coach. • Provide evaluation resources. • Assist with needs assessment. • Assist with goal/outcome identification. • Assist with individual evaluation plan.
Stage 2: Building capacity for action Client's increase *knowledge* of own program strategies and research to support them; *belief* that what they do works; *skill building* in designing and implementing their evaluation.	• Complete logic model. • Concentrate evaluation effort on process development. • Utilize technical assistance. • Maintain momentum despite wanting to give up. • Adopt multiple evaluation strategies to measure process and outcomes.	• Coach and provide feedback, especially when clients feel overwhelmed. • Facilitate process data collection. • Goal/outcome completion. • Logic model revision, completion. • Building evaluation capacity experientially. • Reinforce big-picture frequently.
Stage 3: Taking action More specific evaluation task orientation within program; application of knowledge; beliefs and skill building from Stage 2.	• Collect process data. • Utilize expert help; apply self-correction. • Look for patterns in process data. • Focus on lessons learned. • Complete outcome data collection. • Analyze findings collectively, ask for help. • Write key point summary. • Present to funder.	• Continue big-picture review. • Reinforce lessons learned. • Coach those not up to speed. • Facilitate outcome data collection. • Provide expert direction, as needed. • Advocate with funder, as needed. • Maintain momentum for those who think they are finished.

(continued)

TABLE 9.1. *(continued)*

Stage	Client role	Evaluator role
Stage 4: Refining action Less task orientation; more complex application of skill building and program refinements based on evaluation.	• Revisit big picture. • Apply lessons learned. • Add strategies to build activities. • Disseminate findings. • Publicize program effects. • Develop sustainment plan. • Train others in evaluation.	• Build momentum. • Help clients to refine program. • Facilitate strategic planning. • Facilitate sustainment planning. • Advocate *with* clients and *for* clients.
Stage 5: Institutionalizing action Highly developed evaluation skills including self-efficacy, independence, problem solving, interdependence.	• Increase outreach. • Provide leadership, mentor others. • Build program resources and capacity; help others to do the same. • Initiate wider program efforts into community and beyond. • Use data to sustain project.	• Mentor and help maintain momentum. • Provide sustainment expert direction. • Support cooperative efforts. • Offer ideas for self-sufficiency and sustainment. • Publicize accomplishments outside of community. • Recognize strengths publicly. • Refer others to clients.

evaluation concepts, techniques, and findings to foster improvement and self-determination." Our goal as empowerment evaluators is to build the client's capacity to design and systematically undertake self-assessment at the level of the organization's general capability (Fetterman et al., 2015). Client- and community-driven findings serve as an essential element in management decision making to improve project implementation and outcome effectiveness.

Building capacity may take time to let things play out. In the beginning, waiting to share the data collected by the client is a simple capacity-building tool. For example, completing class fidelity monitoring forms was frustrating for classroom facilitators. Regardless of the site coordinator's training and support, classroom facilitators resisted completing fidelity forms because of the time required given their hourly wage. Rather than admonish sites, we slowed things down by asking people to do their best. At our next evaluation committee meeting, site coordinators reviewed all fidelity data they had collected and on their own revised the fidelity form because they had the time to do so.

Clients determine the ultimate value of their organizational endeavor, not only through a self-assessment, but through continuous quality improvement.[2]

WHAT CHANGES?

Empowerment evaluation changes some standard evaluation elements in ways that have provided significant value to everyone involved, including clients, key stakeholders, and the community. Changes include *who* participates in the assessment, *what* information is gathered and valued, *how* information is handled and interpreted, *when* the assessment process interacts with the course of implementing the project, and the *way* people think.

Empowerment Evaluation Changes *Who* Participates in the Assessment

In this empowerment evaluation, those who funded the project, made up the organization, were key stakeholders, lived in the community, and were funded to complete the project drove the assessment. Any change in the project or the evaluation itself was the collective prerogative of the whole group.

External agents did not impose change. In other words, everyone who shared the risks involved in decision making participated in the assessment. In this highly inclusive process key stakeholders, including the funder, were held accountable for the project outcomes. They made responsible, evidence-based decisions, guided by their evaluation, their own wisdom, and the evaluator's expertise.

> "Our evaluators tell us what they think, but always encourage us to make our own decisions. They do that because we are the ones who must share the risks in making decisions and we are the ones that must live with those decisions. It's about accountability."[3]

This system brought a new perspective and challenge to the work of their evaluation. It also made evaluation more a part of the process of carrying out the project and less of an externally imposed process.

> "We thought we had our mission and our activities figured out and documented in our grant proposal, but our evaluators insisted that

we go through an exercise to redefine them together with the funder. We weren't thrilled. This became a half-day meeting, held in our funder's conference room. The funder's staff attended this session and were careful not to control the process. In retrospect, I know how difficult this must have been for them."

Sites used this opportunity to change their proposal, selecting activities they thought they could collectively accomplish statewide, such as a common mission statement based on the federal guidelines. They also meet quarterly to share community feedback, conduct and refine the assessment, collect and review data, and share accomplishments and challenges. They used a combination of the three-step and 10-step (GTO) approach to conducting the empowerment evaluation.

"Then we did something that we, as clients, had never done before. The evaluators asked all of us to rate from 1 to 10 our status in each of the activities. In other words, they asked for our opinions. After we had individually rated our status, we pooled our results and discussed them. Simple and it worked to pull us together. Then we pursued the remaining GTO steps of project implementation."

Clients oversaw their own assessment. They did not receive formal training to begin the process. They learned by doing and receiving informal training along the way. Because they were doing it themselves in their own context, they also learned that it is a myth that only an evaluator could evaluate a project.

Empowerment Evaluation Changes *What* Information Is Gathered and Valued

Empowerment evaluation is a systematic self-assessment process guided by embedded evaluators, occurring *within* the context of a project (Fetterman et al., 2015). This empowerment evaluation had two standard evaluation components: a process and an outcome assessment.[4] Both elements sought to judge the ultimate value or merit of the endeavor from the client's and the community's viewpoints. Information directly relevant to local decision makers and valued by the group was collected in this comprehensive sex education initiative.

A client- and community-based theory of change and logic model drove this project and evaluation.

"The next step, the development of a logic model, was something we had never heard of before. In hindsight, it was one of the most important activities we completed. A logic model forces you to put your whole project on one sheet of paper. It forces you to explain how you get from theoretical statements to project implementation to impact. Whoa! The logic model sounded *too hard*. We wanted the evaluators to do the logic models. At this point, we kinda wondered what the evaluators get paid to do. We were about to find out. Our evaluators began to teach us, not in formal sessions, but rather through informal meetings and conversations where we practiced *skills* together with the evaluators coaching us. What we learned through practice is that we should be scientific, but not detached, authentic in our findings, but always fixed in the framework that we are the authors of our own development through our evaluation. *With the evaluation committee, then, and with some significant help from our evaluators, we developed our own logic models.*"

Sites started by defining their target population and then described their desired outcomes, followed by activities to accomplish their goals. They defined how they thought comprehensive sex education worked. Their theory of change was based on a combination of their own wisdom and the evaluator's knowledge of how evidence-based, medically accurate, age-appropriate, comprehensive sex education programs reduce unintended teen pregnancy and HIV/STI rates in communities. This was their hybrid theory of change—their story of how comprehensive sex education worked in their context. This provided a framework for accountability measures, specifying activities and outcomes.

"Then we filled in the activities and outcomes. We all learned that results are supposed to be time-specific and measurable. Some of our outcomes were never specified regarding numbers because we were doing something we had never done before and we were unable to make predictions. As time went on and our evaluators helped us focus, we could project reasonable outcomes as a group."

Their evaluation capacity grew exponentially throughout the evaluation.

"Logically explaining how our project works was often a real breakthrough for all of us. Finally, we had a benchmark to measure against.

Our confidence in our own ability to describe and measure what we are undertaking increased considerably. We took more control over our own process and desired outcomes. What empowered us with primary key stakeholders, funders and local decision-makers was to explain not only what worked but why it worked.

"At the same time, we were building infrastructure for two-way capacity building. The evaluators did train us, but it was never formal, except for methods like focus groups or how to develop an interview. And we taught them a lot as well. Even so, we all agreed early on to ask the evaluators to look at our work before we started out on our own. We don't do that now."

The empowerment evaluation also encouraged ongoing data analysis to help people see patterns, gaps, and/or barriers in the project. Now in the fifth year, the state and sites use their statements about lessons learned to refine, judge, and/or revise outcomes.

Empowerment Evaluation Changes *How* to Handle and Interpret Information

In this empowerment evaluation, information was handled and analyzed in a collective and collaborative manner. Information was shared widely. The evaluators coached the funder's, clients', and key stakeholders' discussions about the meaning of their findings to make midcourse adjustments as needed to develop and/or enhance project outcomes. Revising the site's fidelity form three times based on classroom facilitator satisfaction surveys and observations is a good example of a significant midcourse correction, which increased the quality of fidelity reporting.

Collectively, clients, the funder, and key stakeholders associated with the effort analyzed meeting minutes, reviewed evaluator-generated data and reports, and conducted archival studies to enrich outcome data. They conducted learning circles, focus groups, online surveys, and/or one-to-one interviews to determine the merit of their work. After they collected and analyzed their data, they also used infographics shaped by the group to tell their stories. One site consistently analyzed their "big picture" findings. Using the evaluator's site, they developed "Fast Stats," infographics sent bimonthly to each school. These one-page documents simply provided five important findings from each school's data. For example, one infographic pictured a tablet with checkmarks for metrics. Across from the first checkmark was written: "84% of your kids who took the pre–post survey intend to use birth control or a condom if having sex." Across from the second checkmark was written: "17% are less likely to engage in sex in the next 6 months."

They also documented unexpected outcomes. One unexpected finding was from their parent focus groups. Everyone predicted a great deal of blowback from parents regarding sex education that would prevent schools from adopting the program. This did not happen and sites could use this important information with superintendents, school boards, and principals to allay their fears regarding parents. Processes and outcomes that were no longer valid were revised or dropped as clients monitored their own progress. Clients, their funder, key stakeholders, and the evaluators, with community feedback, combined individual data points, analyzed multiple meanings, and synthesized their findings into a collectively developed big picture and then evaluation summary reports.

> "What is important to point out here is that we used several of what the evaluators called 'traditional evaluation methods.' The difference is that we were the source and the collectors of our own data. For example, one of us did regular online assessments of the Askable Adult training and uploaded it to her own database developed by evaluators for her. Another site surveyed local kids and some parents during their sponsored summer events about the need for comprehensive sex education in their rural mountain community."

All evaluation findings were used immediately to inform and influence the community. For example, one site coordinator, in a low-income county, hired 16 interns to set up exhibits at county and health fairs. The interns themselves all had had comprehensive sex education and could answer questions correctly. They handed out small, unmarked brown bags filled with county pregnancy data, birth control/condoms, and abstinence literature. Furthermore, the coordinator had several one-page infographics to explain comprehensive sex education. The interns also had infographics highlighting parental focus group information, focusing on parental approval of local school-based comprehensive sex education to reassure various stakeholders that parents accepted the program. The interns could tell hundreds of residents that most students enjoyed the class, thought the content was relevant and worthwhile, intended to delay sex, and planned to use birth control or condoms if having sex.

Empowerment Evaluation Changes *When* the Assessment Process Interacts with the Course of Implementing the Project

An empowerment evaluation is an ongoing process, with many points of information gathering, rather than an end-of-the-year or end-of-the-grant summation. It guarantees that needed information is part of the project's internal and real-time feedback. During the quarterly evaluation committee meetings, there was extensive data review to problem-solve challenges and revise strategies accordingly. These meetings were supplemented with regular conference calls or video conferences while generating new information. The data collection was richer and more meaningful than typical external efforts because the funder, clients, and key stakeholders, all guided by community feedback, were invested and involved. The richness of the ideas shared stimulated participant's creativity, innovation, and ability to see alternatives. For example, sustainment has been a big issue for coordinators. As a team, they became more budget-conscious. They became more frugal and found more ways to leverage and/or share materials and presentations. Moreover, they influenced program decision making and implementation efforts throughout the project.

Empowerment Evaluation Changes the *Way* People Think

The empowerment evaluation process changes the way people think about their capacity to bring about changes important to them. Not only do they become more self-sufficient and self-efficacious, but they begin to develop ideas about being of service to others. In this case, clients became mentors to others in their community. One site coordinator served as the key resource for community building and evaluation when a group in her county was awarded a sizeable grant from Communities That Care. She helped set up key contacts and share evaluation strategies from GTO. Researchers refer to this far-reaching empowerment as interactional and behavioral, that is, between persons and their environment that enable them to successfully master their social or political systems (Terborg, 1981). The results experienced by this group were consistent with this theory, specifically including institutionalizing evaluation to facilitate effective community change.

> "Evaluation has now been institutionalized in our work as a state collaborative and into projects that are outside the collaborative. For

example, we integrated evaluation data to change class length in our schools. Our classes were often longer than a typical class schedule. We used our data to show school administrators what the program can do when taught as designed. We were also able to demonstrate that shorter classes were not working for our kids. This is a big hurdle to overcome as other classes were affected. But we worked it out per each school's needs. If we did not have data showing positive outcomes, we might not have been able to do this."

Empowerment evaluation helped people to think like evaluators, relying on data to inform decision making and institutionalizing the process to establish this way of thinking as an organizational norm (Fetterman, 2013a).

LESSONS LEARNED

The empowerment evaluators in this endeavor learned valuable lessons. They included issues associated with front-end demands and costs, rigor, causation, levels of abstraction, communication, and resistance.

Front-End Demands and Costs

Time, money, and intensive coaching were necessary at the beginning of this project and evaluation. It helped to build participant's competence, confidence, and knowledge slowly at first. Because clients' and key stakeholders' skills, levels of commitment, and motivation varied, the beginning of the project was the most challenging aspect of the undertaking. Some did not recognize the benefit of participation until much later in the project. Once the evaluation was underway and client involvement in the evaluation increased, the costs decreased significantly. The comprehensive sex education program clients indicated that the initial investment was worthwhile.

Rigor Was Not Lost

Clients who were responsible for data collection, data management, and other activities at the "front line" of the evaluation understood from the beginning to the end of the evaluation the importance of following agreed-upon protocols and standard operating procedures. However, the empowerment evaluator was responsible for clients' understanding of the evaluation framework, in this case primarily GTO. Rigor improved as clients' skills and commitment increased.

Knowing Why It Happened

Empowerment evaluations strive to show patterns in the data. Clients in this comprehensive sex education initiative were encouraged to explain in everyday terms both what happened and why it happened. For example, one site had lower content knowledge than others. The coordinator looked at the site coordinator's data and knew that she had a problem when she compared her data to statewide data, but did not know why. We encouraged her to look at her fidelity data again and then she found that several high school kids were special education youth who were struggling in regular comprehensive sex education classes. She worked with the school to have all the special education youth instructed together with a revised curriculum by a retired special education teacher.

Evaluators helped clients learn how to compare results across sites. This enabled them to make convincing arguments about why things were happening across the state. For example, several site evaluations identified a lack of community engagement in planning as a key factor to successfully reducing unintended teen pregnancy, not only in schools, but at the community level as well. To increase their reliability, a sustained effort was required to work together on joint analyses of the data (with empowerment evaluation coaching).

Difficulties Arise When Theoretical Models Are Used

Clients displayed everyday wisdom throughout the project. However, the majority did not see the significance of complex theoretical models used to link events and/or data. Periodically, clients needed evaluative assistance to suggest analytical relationships and see the bigger picture. They also helped differentiate between levels of abstraction throughout the evaluation.

Clients May Not Be Able to Explain Why Their Project Produces Few Effects

Clients were occasionally at a loss to explain why "things weren't changing" the way they expected or understood. Coaching people to trust their instincts and look for patterns in the data helped lessen some of their anxiety at practicing their newly acquired evaluation skills. It also increased their understanding of indirect changes and outcomes. The empowerment evaluators worked with the clients to help put the pieces together to facilitate the process and draw a picture of the larger pattern. Ultimately, however, the crystallizing moments were the clients' right and responsibility. (See Fetterman, 2017, concerning the locus of control or role of staff and community members in crystallizing their own understandings and insights in empowerment evaluation.) The empowerment evaluators also aggregated and disaggregated the data with clients to bridge this gap in understanding and attribution. The empowerment evaluators offered their interpretations of the data, but they always put the participant wisdom at the forefront, even when the clients were unclear about the overall impact of the initiative.

Constant, Ongoing, and Frequent Communications[5]

Constant, ongoing, and frequent communications were mandatory in this initiative. The need for planned, regular, and clear communication between funders, evaluators, and clients with key stakeholders and clients within the community was critical. It helped people remain focused and minimized misunderstandings. It also improved the management of the evaluation and the project.

The empowerment evaluators set a tone for the evaluation, in part by creating a "safe zone" for open and productive discussions. Meaningful and planned communication enhanced community awareness concerning day-to-day progress of the evaluation. It also improved a meaningful interpretation of data.

Resistance

Most of the clients were fully engaged in the evaluation. However, they did not have the knowledge or skills to conduct the evaluation by themselves. Coaching was invaluable in those cases. Others did not have the time and/or interest to participate in the evaluation. Coaxing was helpful, as was peer pressure. However, there were some clients and members of the community who simply refused to get involved, preferring the safety of the sidelines or total noninvolvement. In those cases, the focus of the effort had to remain with the group committed and engaged and only secondarily on recruiting those resistant to change and engagement.

CONCLUSION

There are no magic wands, no hidden tricks, no secret handshakes, or similar mystique to evaluation. It is a myth that "only an evaluator can do it." Ordinary people have the capacity to conduct their own evaluations, with the assistance of trained evaluators, as well as established processes, such as Fetterman's three-step and Wandersman's 10-step GTO approaches (see Chinman et al., 2008; Fetterman, 2015; Wandersman, Imm, Chinman, & Kaftarian, 2000).

Empowerment evaluations are a gateway to growth in human potential, capacity, and self-determination. People grow in their ability to take control of their own lives and improve the conditions that affect them. Often the most meaningful changes are those that occur in our daily routine. They can be linked to an increase in capacity to initiate and carry out social transformation. This chapter highlights only one empowerment evaluation. It had a significant impact on many levels. For example:

1. Greater empowerment and integration of resources across the community and state that opened doors for clients to reach out to others, especially those that had the power to help them implement the program in schools where administrators and school boards were reluctant to implement comprehensive sex education classes.

2. Increased client- and community-driven strategies to start building the much-needed social infrastructure for comprehensive sex education classes.

3. Establishment of relationships that facilitated more effective state- and countywide unintended teen pregnancy prevention.

4. Increased individual and collective interest in and engagement with project programs.

5. Greater resiliency of the funder, clients, and project staff as they realized there was community support and that together they could grow and sustain project programs.

These are significant outcomes. They were dependent in large part upon building evaluation capacity. Evaluation capacity building is required to make large-scale and long-term differences in communities. It is one of empowerment evaluation's most significant contributions to social change and development.

NOTES

1. See also Zimmerman (2000).

2. See GTO Step 9.

3. The quotations are summaries of several voices. They represent a collective voice based on a comprehensive series of interviews.

4. These self-assessments and judgments not only address the project accomplishments, implementation, and outcomes, but also other equally important formative factors, such as (a) examination of the chronological sequence of project planning and implementation; (b) analysis of project structure, components, and delivery systems; (c) a better understanding of contextual factors in which the project was taking place; (d) whether the outcomes and project design made sense in reality; (e) participation rates and engagement characteristics; (f) perception of project clients; (g) levels of community awareness; (h) resources used for project operation; and (i) an analysis of unplanned results, as well as the planned ones.

5. Much effort in an empowerment evaluation is spent building and maintaining relationships. This is accomplished, in part, by sharing perspectives and joint evaluation activities.

CHAPTER 10

A Google-Enhanced Empowerment Evaluation Approach in a Graduate School Program

David M. Fetterman and Jason Ravitz

Empowerment evaluation can assume many shapes and forms. For example, there is a three-step approach and a 10-step GTO model, both described earlier in Chapters 8 and 9. Google has developed a strategy for planning evaluation using a series of worksheets and resources that can enhance or provide another approach to empowerment evaluation. This chapter demonstrates the power of empowerment evaluation to create a shared vision, and the strength of Google's technologies and evaluation worksheets to improve practice and provide additional specificity, as is typically associated with rigorous evaluation.

In this chapter, we discuss how this combined approach is being exported to higher education, specifically use of empowerment evaluation to evaluate a doctoral program at Pacifica Graduate Institute by its own graduate students. The lessons learned from this experiment are being reflexively mirrored back to Google to improve their evaluation capacity-building efforts with the nonprofits and initiatives they support. Our work enhances the three-step empowerment evaluation approach by adding more specific evaluation tools and technologies designed at Google to build evaluation capacity and improve outreach efforts.

GOOGLE

Google is one of the most recognized company names in the world, largely known for its search engine. A part of its mission is "to organize the world's information and make it universally accessible and useful." It is also known for many of its "moon shots" like the self-driving car, Internet-beaming hot air balloons, and a pill that can detect cancer.

Google is also committed to outreach and investing in education, with an emphasis on increasing interest in careers in computer science among underrepresented minorities and women. Google is exploring ways to use principles and practices from empowerment evaluation to improve its evaluation infrastructure and increase the impact of its outreach programs.

Training has been provided within Google, both in-person (Figure 10.1) and online, using Google Hangouts. It has also been offered to higher education institutions and nonprofits, as discussed below.

FIGURE 10.1. Jason Ravitz and David Fetterman developing their enhanced empowerment evaluation approach at Google.

PACIFICA GRADUATE INSTITUTE

The Pacifica Graduate Institute is an accredited graduate school offering masters' and doctoral degree programs in depth psychology (see Figure 10.2). Their empowerment evaluation course offered an opportunity to apply the three-step approach to empowerment evaluation, described in Chapters 8 and 9, and to add Google's evaluation worksheets (described below). In addition, we further enhanced the three-step approach to empowerment evaluation by adding an online feedback and review component. This mini-experiment has provided insights into the power of rubrics and technology to guide the self-assessment process and create more opportunities for empowerment within and across communities of learners[1] (see Ravitz & Hoadley, 2005). Our shared efforts demonstrated the value of using multiple tools to enhance empowerment evaluation.

WHY EMPOWERMENT EVALUATION?

Empowerment evaluation provides a strategy for using data and evidence for decision making. This is consistent with Google's data-driven culture. Empowerment evaluation can contribute to this culture by helping people to develop a shared vision before they collect or analyze data. Empowerment evaluation helps people learn to think like an evaluator, developing evaluation capacity and helping create an *evaluation-driven* culture.

Google also invests in a multitude of educational outreach initiatives (e.g., the RISE awards at *go.co/csedu*, Google.org, or the CS OPEN project, discussed below). Empowerment evaluation complement's Google's efforts in the nonprofit space because it provides strategies for building evaluation capacity, especially for creating a shared vision for how metrics can be useful. Empowerment evaluation has been used to support elementary, secondary, and postsecondary institutions, as well as in nonprofit community-based organizations and for corporate philanthropic educational initiatives such as those created at Google.

Finally, Google's K–12 outreach team has invested in evaluation capacity building to help nonprofit organizations and universities monitor and assess their own performance. Empowerment evaluation is designed to help people and organizations build evaluation capacity. We share the goals of building capacity, and we want to do this by cultivating learning

FIGURE 10.2. Pacifica Graduate Institute students using empowerment evaluation steps to assess their program.

communities and learning organizations. Our aim is to help organizations, communities, and classrooms use evaluation to improve performance and accomplish their goals.

APPLICATION OF EMPOWERMENT EVALUATION

Pacifica Graduate Institute doctoral students used the three-step empowerment evaluation approach to assess their own program, including (1) mission, (2) taking stock, and (3) planning for the future. They also created an evaluation dashboard to monitor their performance, comparing their actual performance with their goals and milestones. Their recommendations, based on their plans for the future, were shared with faculty in an effort to recruit support to improve their program, ranging from changes in the syllabi to increasing student and faculty diversity. (As discussed earlier, empowerment evaluation has been used in a number of accreditation self-studies in part because it ensures participation and increases the probabilities of producing desired results [Fetterman, 2012; Fetterman et al., 2010].)

In addition, the doctoral students assessed their own performance and their peers' performance in the empowerment evaluation course. Specifically, they were required to produce an empowerment evaluation proposal. The proposals have been used in the past to conduct empowerment evaluations, solicit funding, and/or to guide doctoral dissertations.

The proposals for this course included a description of the three-step process planned to assess their program's performance, as well as an evaluation dashboard to monitor their progress. This created a shared evaluation vision for the organizations, agencies, and programs (and a measure of accountability). Additional specificity, provided by the Google evaluation worksheets, improved their capacity to conduct an empowerment evaluation.

GOOGLE EVALUATION WORKSHEETS

The Google evaluation worksheets provide the group with the opportunity to be more specific about their evaluation plans (Figure 10.3). It helps them clarify purposes, relationships, duties, responsibilities, methods, and contextual variables. There are four worksheet parts. The first asked the group to describe the program to be evaluated.

Questions included:

- "What is the overall program purpose?"
- "Whom does the program serve?"
- "Who else is involved or invested in the success of the program?"
- "What does the program do?"
- "What are the immediate and short-term outcomes?"
- "What are the longer-term outcomes?"

The second part asked the group to define the evaluation context. Questions included the following:

- "Why are you evaluating?"
- "Who are the audiences for the evaluation?"
- "What do you really want to know? What is the focus of evaluation?"
- "How will the results be utilized, and by whom?"
- "Are there other contextual factors that influence the evaluation?"

The third part was designed to elicit information to help plan the evaluation. Questions included:

- "What are the key evaluation questions?"
- "Who are participants in the evaluation?"
- "What methods will you use to collect the data?"
- "Will you use existing data instruments/tools or create your own?"
- "How will you analyze and draw conclusions?"

The fourth part addressed creating an evaluation management plan. Questions focused on the following areas: team description and roles, reporting, budget, management plan, and timeline.

These worksheets compel the group to, for example, state who the audiences are, list key questions, describe the methods they will use, and specify what they are going to do. This approach, which builds on lessons from graduate evaluation courses created by Nick L. Smith at Syracuse University, helps to maximize their efforts and minimize missed steps.

Describe Program

Part A: Describe the Program to Be Evaluated

What is the overall program purpose?
Is a primary purpose or need addressed? Are there secondary purposes or needs? (More info)

Whom does the program serve?
Who are the primary and secondary participants? Who benefits directly and indirectly (e.g., students and their families or communities) (More info)

Who else is involved or invested in the success of the program?
(e.g., key stakeholders such as funders, boards, staff, parents, community members, partner organizations)

What does the program do?
What are the main activities? Who delivers it? How do people participate (e.g., online, face-to-face)? How often and how long does it run (e.g., contact hours)? (More info)

What are the immediate and short-term outcomes?
What happens as an immediate result of the program? (More info)

What are the longer-term outcomes?
What happens over the longer term as a result of the program? (More info)

Define Evaluation

Part B: Define the Evaluation Context (Purpose, Audience)

Why are you evaluating? (e.g., development of the program, accountability, testing a theory, or learning) (More info)

Who are the audiences for the evaluation?
Who is paying for the evaluation? Who are the primary and secondary audiences who will see the results, care, or be impacted by them? (often the program funder and/or stakeholders) (More info)

What do you really want to know? What is the focus of evaluation?
You can't look at everything. Is the key issue program design, activities, delivery, outcomes, etc.? (More info)

How will the results be utilized, and by whom? (e.g., improving, informing, deciding, guiding, etc.)

Are there other contextual factors that influence the evaluation?
What else may influence your results? (e.g., new policies, initiatives, another study, etc.) (More info)

FIGURE 10.3. Google evaluation worksheets (Ravitz & Fetterman, 2016).

Management Plan

Part D: Create an Evaluation Management Plan

Team Description and Roles
Who plays what role? Who leads and what does that include? What will staff handle? What are the qualifications of those involved? What relationships exist and will be created? (More info)

Reporting
What needs to be reported, to whom, when? What will the format of each report be? How will you share interim and final findings differently? (see template below or more info)

Budget
What is a breakdown of costs and resources used for the evaluation, including staff time by level? What are costs for travel, materials, supplies, etc.? (More info/Templates)

Management Plan and Timeline
What is the evaluation task list, timeline, and responsibilities? (More info)

Plan Evaluation

Part C: Plan the Evaluation (Questions, Data Sources, Procedures)

What are the key evaluation questions?
What are the specific questions you will spend your time and resources answering? (More info)

Who are participants in the evaluation?
Whose perspectives or data will you include? How will participants be selected? (More info)

What methods will you use to collect the data? (e.g., field work, surveys, interviews, observations, etc.) (More info)

Will you use existing data instruments/tools or create your own?
What measures are already available? What will you have to collect yourself? How can you partner with the program to streamline data collection and make it more useful? (More info)

How will you analyze and draw conclusions?
What analytics will you use, how will you use them to set criteria and make judgments? (More info)

FIGURE 10.3. *(continued)*

In the context of empowerment evaluation, answering these questions makes the self-evaluation more efficient, potentially more rigorous, and more likely to remain on target. It also permits larger studies to be proposed and funded, and makes sure these are conducted with staff buy-in, simultaneously addressing concerns about bias, rigor, and accountability.

RUBRICS: GOOBRICS, GOOBRICS FOR STUDENTS, AND GOOGLE FORMS

One of the requirements of the class was to assess their own evaluation proposals and their peers' proposals. They used the feedback, along with the instructor's assessment, to refine and improve their final product. The class met face to face, but a virtual classroom *strategy*, proposed by Ravitz and Hoadley (2005), was added to facilitate the peer review and assessment. This improved the quality of the proposals before they were reviewed by the instructors, and modeled the course focus on empowerment evaluation and capacity building. It also helped the instructors reinforce what was learned and adapt instruction to address misconceptions or missed concepts.

The class used Google Docs, an online word-processing program, to draft their proposals, facilitating peer and instructor access. The doctoral students posted their proposals online in the cloud using Doctopus, a group or classroom management software (Figure 10.4). These two

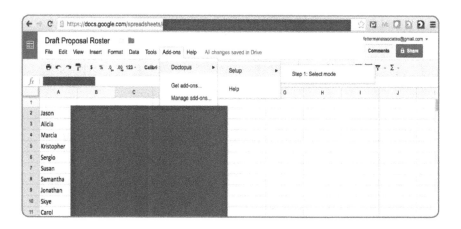

FIGURE 10.4. Using Doctopus to manage student files online.

programs enabled students to access each other's proposals (once invited) and for the instructors to keep track of all the proposals in one place.

The instructors used rubrics to provide additional guidance for proposal development and review. Rubrics are criteria used to guide instruction and assessment. Students were asked to rate on a 1 (low) to 5 (high) scale how well their peers discussed topics or activities in their proposals, specifically related to the three-step empowerment evaluation process and the four evaluation parts of the worksheets.

They used Goobrics and Goobrics for Students (Chrome browser extensions) as well as Google Forms (a survey software) to rate their own work and their peers' proposals (Figure 10.5). With the press of a button on their screen, the rubrics appear on top of the proposal being reviewed, appearing as a menu of topics with cells for their ratings (Figure 10.6). They rated their proposals based on categories such as description of the theory of change, use of a critical friend, as well as standard concerns such as budget, reporting, and timeline. The "comments" section of Google Docs provided an opportunity for more detailed feedback.

The power of rubrics was compelling when the self-, peer-, and instructor ratings were compared. (Concerning the validity of online self-ratings, see Kaplan & Bornet, 2014; Topping, 1998; Wagner, Churl Suh, & Cruz, 2011.) We found that the self-, peer, and instructor assessments

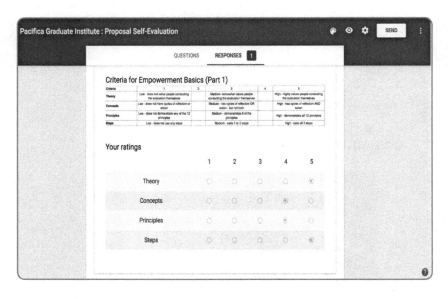

FIGURE 10.5. Students using Google Forms to assess self and peers.

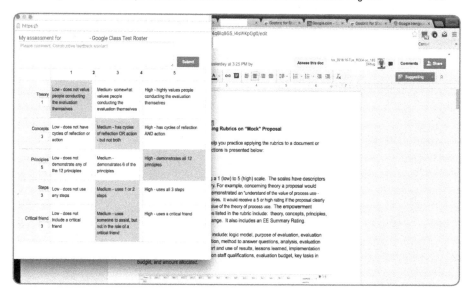

FIGURE 10.6. Rubric to guide student self- and peer assessment (using Goobric for Students software).

were closely aligned, highlighting effective communication and learning (Figure 10.7). The ratings also helped identify areas meriting additional attention before the course concluded.

Together these online feedback and review programs enabled students to critique both their own proposals and each other's work conveniently, while maintaining instructional supervision. Rubrics and their resulting data were used to guide both learning and instruction. We believe adding technology in this case is a further enhancement of empowerment evaluation because it is free, encourages collaboration, and is not restricted to any single institution. In addition, it can be replicated to help groups evaluate themselves.

CONCLUSION

Empowerment evaluation is used in a wide variety of contexts and settings. In addition, there is no single set of tools required to conduct an empowerment evaluation. It should be guided by specific principles (described in Chapter 8), including improvement, respect for community

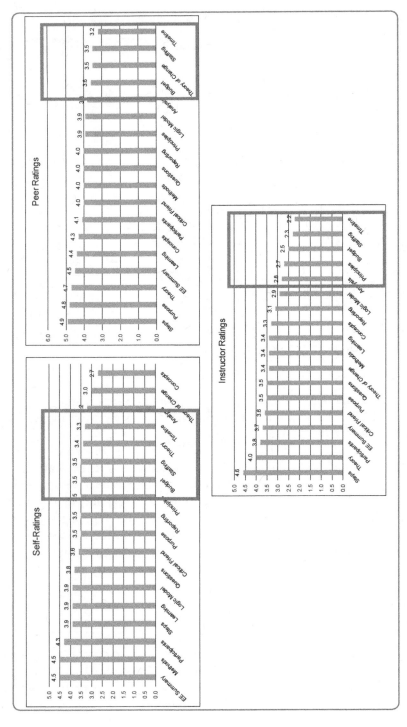

FIGURE 10.7. Self-, peer, and instructor evaluations (demonstrating convergence of ratings).

knowledge, capacity building, organizational learning, and accountability. However, in this case a three-step process was combined with an evaluation worksheet approach. The combination was synergistic. The three-step process helped create a shared vision. The worksheets allowed people to drill down and specify the who, what, when, and where of an evaluation.

The work does not end here. We are learning from each application how to refine and improve practice, and this is influencing our work in empowerment evaluation, at Google and with other nonprofits as well. Through the Computer Science Outreach Program Evaluation Network (CS OPEN) Google has funded and provided technical assistance to 12 nonprofits through a partnership with the National Girls Collaborative Project. As the lessons we are learning influence programs such as these, we will see more real-life examples that demonstrate the power and utility of empowerment evaluation and its ever-evolving toolbox to support and foster self-determination.

NOTE

1. Students use these online tools to give peer feedback to help refine and improve their proposals: Goobric (software to facilitate group assessment of performance by individuals), Goobric for Students, and Google Forms (software to facilitate self-, peer-, and leader or instructor assessments).

CHAPTER 11

Similarities across the Three Approaches

Principles and Practices in Common

David M. Fetterman, Liliana Rodríguez-Campos,
Abraham Wandersman, Rita Goldfarb O'Sullivan,
and Ann P. Zukoski

Collaborative, participatory, and empowerment evaluations have definite clear distinctions that separate them, as discussed in previous chapters. However, in many respects these approaches have more in common than the differences that distinguish them from each other. Principles and practices, including methods, represent "common threads" uniting these approaches.

This chapter presents the principles guiding each approach and highlights principles in common. In addition, the results of the AEA's CPE-TIG panels and surveys, focusing on guiding principles, are discussed. Other guiding principles are presented, as well as these independent efforts. They have provided useful guidance. However, there is merit in organizing and unifying these separate threads.

A macro-, mid-, or microlevel of analysis is used to organize these principles. The resulting synthesis of these lists is presented to inform the use of these guiding principles. A brief discussion about shared methods and skills further demonstrates the similarities across approaches. This chapter demonstrates how similar principles, methods, and skills unite and define each approach.

COLLABORATIVE, PARTICIPATORY, AND EMPOWERMENT EVALUATION PRINCIPLES

Each approach has articulated a set of guiding principles[1] (in varying degrees of detail, thoroughness, and consistency). They are used to inform evaluation practice. The principles have been extracted primarily from the "essentials" chapters and are presented in Boxes 11.1–11.3 for comparative purposes.

Box 11.1. Collaborative Evaluation Principles

1. *Development*—the use of training (such as workshops or seminars) or any other mechanism (e.g., mentoring) to enhance learning and self-improvement.

2. *Empathy*—the display of sensitivity, understanding, and a thoughtful response toward the feelings or emotions of others, therefore better managing a positive reaction to your collaborative environment.

3. *Empowerment*—the development of a sense of self-efficacy by delegating authority and removing any possible obstacles (such as inadequate feelings) that might limit the attainment of established goals.

4. *Involvement*—the constructive combination of forces (complementing each other's strengths and weaknesses) throughout the collaboration in a way that is feasible and meaningful for everyone: the level of involvement varies among everyone who collaborates in the effort.

5. *Qualification*—the level of knowledge and skills needed to achieve an effective collaboration; it is the preparation for dealing with relevant performance issues that is directly affected by the individual's background.

6. *Social support*—the management of relationships with others in order to establish a sense of belonging and a holistic view of social-related issues; it is the ability to develop productive networks in order to find solutions in a collaborative way.

7. *Trust*—the firm confidence in or reliance on the sincerity, credibility, and reliability of everyone involved in the collaboration; although a high level of trust must exist for a successful collaboration, trust takes time to build and can be eliminated easily.

Source: Rodríguez-Campos and Rincones-Gómez (2013).

Box 11.2. Participatory Evaluation Principles

1. *Participant focus and ownership.* Participatory evaluation seeks to create structures and processes to engage and create ownership among all key stakeholders. The process seeks to honor the perspectives, voices, and knowledge of those most impacted, including program participants or recipients, who are often voiceless in the evaluation process. *Sources:* USAID (1996) and Institute of Development Studies (1998).

2. *Negotiation and balance of power.* Participants commit to work together to decide on the evaluation approach. There is a balance of power among team members and the evaluator to determine each step of the evaluation process.

3. *Learning.* Participants learn together about what is working about a program and what is not, and together determine what actions are needed to improve program outcomes.

4. *Flexibility.* The evaluation approach will change based on resources, needs, and skills of participants. *Source:* Guijt and Gaventa (1998, pp. 2–4).

5. *Focus on action planning.* The main purpose of participatory evaluation is to identify points of action to improve program implementation. *Sources:* U.S. Agency for International Development (1996) and Institute of Development Studies (1998, pp. 2–3, 5).

6. *Sharing control.* Everyone involved in the program shares control over the evaluation process.

7. *Objectives set jointly.* The objectives are set jointly, in a group, with all the people concerned in the program, keeping in mind that everyone has his or her own agenda.

8. *Work out difficulties together.* Working out the difficulties faced by everyone helps in strengthening the program.

9. *Awareness raising.* There is a process of collective awareness raising. *Source:* Crishna (2006, pp. 6–9).

Principles in Common

A review of each of the approaches' principles highlights substantial underlying similarities. For example, explicitly they share many of the same principles, including involvement, participant focus, capacity building, valuing community knowledge, learning, and improvement (see Figure 11.1). In addition, depending on the circumstances and context, they each may share principles of empowerment[2] and social justice. Implicitly, they share the following principles: trust, ownership, qualifications, empathy/sympathy, and democratic participation. (See Appendix 11.1.)

Box 11.3. Empowerment Evaluation Principles

1. *Improvement.* Empowerment evaluation is intended to help people improve program performance; it is designed to help people build on their successes and reevaluate areas meriting attention.

2. *Community ownership.* Empowerment evaluation values and facilitates community control; use and sustainability are dependent on a sense of ownership.

3. *Inclusion.* Empowerment evaluation invites involvement, participation, and diversity; contributions come from all levels and walks of life.

4. *Democratic participation.* Participation and decision making should be open and fair.

5. *Social justice.* Evaluation can and should be used to address social inequities in society.

6. *Community knowledge.* Empowerment evaluation respects and values community knowledge.

7. *Evidence-based strategies.* Empowerment evaluation respects and uses the knowledge base of scholars (in conjunction with community knowledge).

8. *Capacity building.* Empowerment evaluation is designed to enhance stakeholders' ability to conduct evaluation and to improve program planning and implementation.

9. *Organizational learning.* Data should be used to evaluate new practices, inform decision making, and implement program practices; empowerment evaluation is used to help organizations learn from their experience (building on successes, learning from mistakes, and making midcourse corrections).

10. *Accountability.* Empowerment evaluation is focused on outcomes and accountability; empowerment evaluation functions within the context of existing policies, standards, and measures of accountability; did the program or initiative accomplish its objectives?

Source: Fetterman and Wandersman (2015).

CPE-TIG-Generated Lists of Principles

The AEA's CPE-TIG held several conference sessions over a 5-year period to focus on "features in common." They generated a list of principles associated with each approach, highlighting the most important principles guiding their work. This list of principles is evolving and will continue to be revised over time. The list of principles with their corresponding definitions are provided below:

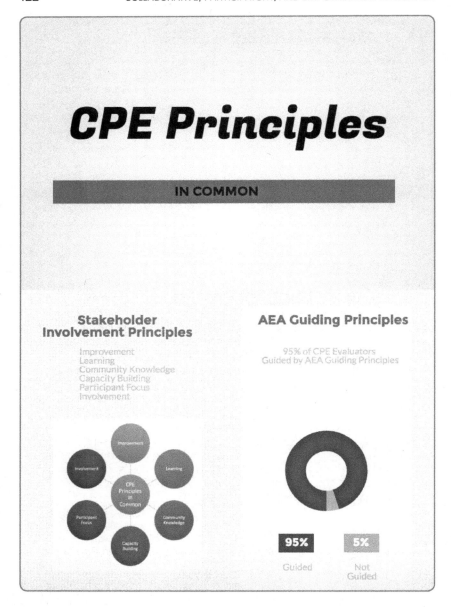

FIGURE 11.1. Infographic of CPE Principles in common, including stakeholder involvement principles and AEA Guiding Principles. See Appendix 11.1 for a detailed comparison of principles across stakeholder-involvement approaches to evaluation. Courtesy of David M. Fetterman.

- *Accountability*—focus on outcomes and accountability; did the program or initiative accomplish its objectives?
- *Capacity building*—enhance stakeholders' ability to conduct evaluation and to improve program planning and implementation
- *Community knowledge*—respect and value community knowledge
- *Community ownership*—value and facilitate community control; assume use and sustainability are dependent on a sense of ownership
- *Competence*—possess knowledge, skills, and attitudes required to conduct stakeholder involvement approaches to evaluation; have appropriate qualifications
- *Democratic participation*—ensure that participation and decision making are open and fair
- *Empathy*—demonstrate sensitivity and understanding concerning the feelings of others
- *Empowerment*—help people take control over their own lives, promote self-efficacy
- *Evaluation use*—help people use evaluation to inform decision making, program planning and implementation, and strategic planning
- *Evidence-based strategies*—respect and use the knowledge base of scholars (in conjunction with community knowledge)
- *Improvement*—help people improve program performance; help people build on their successes and reevaluate areas meriting attention
- *Involvement*—invite involvement, participation, and diversity; assume contributions come from all levels and walks of life
- *Organizational learning*—use data to evaluate new practices, inform decision making, and implement program practices; use evaluation to help organizations learn from their experience (building on successes, learning from mistakes, and making midcourse corrections)
- *Self-determination*[3]—help people make choices and decisions based on their own preferences and interests, to monitor and regulate their own actions and to become goal-oriented and self-directing

- *Social justice*—make sure that evaluation can and should be used to address social inequities in society
- *Social support*—cultivate a sense of solidarity and belonging to enhance capacity to work productively together as group
- *Sustainability*—focus on helping people to continue their work for the long term (beyond an initial pilot program or receipt of seed money)
- *Trust*—treat people honestly, fairly, and reliably to build relationships such that people can take risks and depend on each other

CPE-TIG Survey Results

CPE-TIG conducted a survey of its membership based on this list of "most important" guiding principles. Principles held in common across approaches (70–92% in agreement) included the following: capacity building, improvement, evaluation use, trust, organizational learning, community knowledge, accountability, empathy, evidence-based practices, and sustainability. Principles held in common at the 45–66% level included social justice, democratic participation, community ownership, competence, empowerment, social support, and self-determination (see Figure 11.2).

An additional list of principles and attributes guiding the membership (based on the survey results) included equity, accessibility, results, culturally competent, integrity, fairness, standards, diversity, open communication, resilience, ethics, transformative, transparency, respect, accuracy, collaborative, humility, courage, engagement, and humor.

The majority of collaborative, participatory, and empowerment evaluators (95%) stated they were also guided by the AEA's Guiding Principles (see Figure 11.1). In addition, collaborative evaluation and empowerment evaluation explicitly adhere to the spirit of the Joint Committee on Standards for Educational Evaluation (1994), concerning utility, feasibility, propriety, and accuracy (see Fetterman, 2001b, pp. 87–99).

Additional Guiding Principles

There are many additional useful guiding principles related to stakeholder involvement approaches to evaluation, including the International Radiation Protection Association's (2012) Guiding Principles for Radiation Protection Professionals on Stakeholder Engagement; Petts

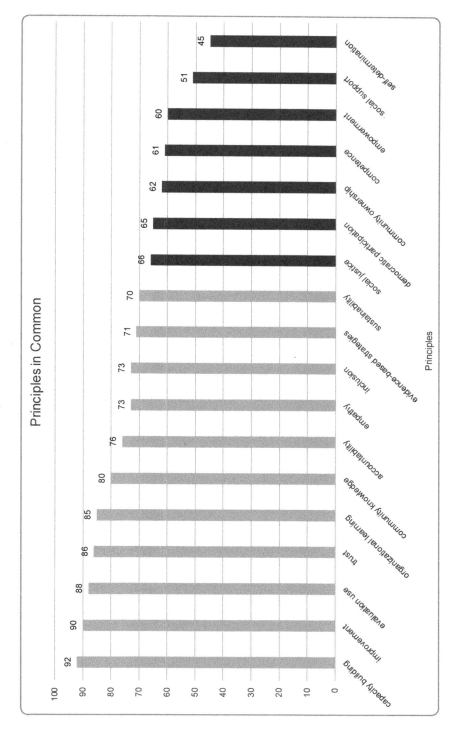

FIGURE 11.2. Survey results concerning principles held in common across approaches.

and Leach's (2000) Principles of Engagement; and the Co-Intelligence Institute's (2008) Principles to Nurture Wise Democratic Process and Collective Intelligence in Public Participation.

Another study concerning principles associated with stakeholder involvement approaches to evaluation identified a brief list that merits attention (Shulha, Whitmore, Cousins, Gilbert, & al Hudib, 2016). These principles are "intended to yield guidance rather than direction" (p. 196). The principles and corresponding assembled definitions (from Cousins, Whitmore, Shulha, al Hudib, & Gilbert, 2015) are provided below:

- *Clarify motivation for collaboration*—encourages the development of a thorough understanding of the justification for the collaborative approach.

- *Foster meaningful relationships*—inspires the conscious development of quality working relationships between evaluators and program stakeholders and among stakeholders, including open and frequent communication.

- *Develop a shared understanding of the program*—promotes the explication of the program logic situated within context.

- *Promote appropriate participatory processes*—encourages deliberate reflection on the form that the collaborative process will take in practice with regard to specific roles and responsibilities for the range of stakeholders identified for participation.

- *Monitor and respond to resource availability*—warrants serious attention to the extent to which stakeholder evaluation team members are unencumbered by competing demands from their regular professional roles.

- *Monitor evaluation progress and quality*—underscores the critical importance of data quality assurance and the maintenance of professional standards of evaluation practice.

- *Promote evaluative thinking*—inspires the active and conscious development of an organizational cultural appreciation for evaluation and its power to leverage social change.

- *Follow-through to realize use*—promotes the conscious consideration of the potential for learning, capacity building, and other practical and transformative consequences of the evaluation. Implicated are evaluation processes and findings.

SYNTHESIZING PRINCIPLES

There are a great variety of principles guiding stakeholder involvement approaches to evaluation. Moreover, most of the principles discussed to date are reinforcing and supportive of each other. The synergistic sum of reinforcing principles is greater than any individual set of principles. They also operate along a continuum of emphasis, depending on the nature and circumstances associated with the evaluation, evaluator, community member, and funder. They can be applied at high, medium, and low levels of commitment (depending on the need and context). (See Fetterman, 2005b, for an example of different levels of commitment in empowerment evaluation.) Each of the approaches continues to evolve and change over time. Thus, one fruitful approach is to consider these principles as different levels of analysis, rather than as conflicting or competing guidelines.

Levels of Analysis

The proliferation of guiding principles presented above is more useful once viewed in terms of levels of analysis. Guiding principles can be organized according to macro-, mid-, and microlevels of analysis. The macrolevel is useful for overall and general guidance. The midlevel is typically associated with a subset of a population, or special interest groups, such as groups associated with qualitative and quantitative methods; infographics and data visualization; and stakeholder involvement approaches to evaluation. The microlevel of analysis refers to one part of a midlevel group, such as collaborative evaluation, participatory evaluation, or empowerment evaluation.

Macrolevel Principles

Principles empirically derived across diverse groups might be viewed as the macrolevel of analysis. For example, the AEA's (2004) Guiding Principles for Evaluators help to guide an entire profession and focus on systematic inquiry, competence, integrity/honesty, respect for people, and responsibility for general and public welfare. Similarly, the Australasian Evaluation Society's guidelines for the ethical conduct of evaluation discuss commissioning and preparing for an evaluation; conducting an evaluation; and reporting the results of an evaluation (go to *https://www. aes.asn.au/images/stories/files/About/Documents%20-%20ongoing/AES%20*

Guidlines10.pdf). The Canadian Evaluation Society provides ethical guidelines concerning competence, integrity, and accountability (visit *www.evaluationcanada.ca/program-evaluation-standards*). The Caribbean Evaluators International speaks in terms of shared core values, highlighting ethical behavior, excellence, professionalism, inclusiveness, and transparency (go to *www.caribbeanevaluatorsinternational.org/evaluation-standards-and-guidelines-embracedby-the-cei.html*). Similarly, the South African Monitoring and Evaluation Association promotes high-quality intellectual, ethical, and professional standards (visit *www.samea.org.za/samea-54.phtml*).

Midlevel Principles

Midlevel principles are designed to guide a subset of a population. For example, the International Radiation Protection Association (IRPA; 2012) issued the *IRPA Guiding Principles for Radiation Protection Professionals on Stakeholder Engagement*. Remove the radiation focus and their principles are particularly pertinent concerning stakeholder engagement. They include (1) identify opportunities for engagement and ensure the level of engagement is proportionate to the nature of the radiation protection issues and their context; (2) initiate the process as early as possible, and develop a sustainable implementation plan; (3) enable an open, inclusive, and transparent stakeholder engagement process; (4) seek out and involve relevant stakeholders and experts; (5) ensure that the roles and responsibilities of all participants and the rules for cooperation are clearly defined; (6) collectively develop objectives for the stakeholder engagement process, based on a shared understanding of issues and boundaries; (7) develop a culture that values a shared language and understanding, and favors collective learning; (8) respect and value the expression of different perspectives; (9) ensure a regular feedback mechanism is in place to inform and improve current and future stakeholder engagement processes; and (10) apply the IRPA Code of Ethics in their actions within these processes to the best of their knowledge.

In addition, Petts and Leach (2000) developed Principles of Engagement, which are applicable to stakeholder involvement approaches to evaluation. They include (1) a need for clarity of objectives, and of legal, linked, and seamless processes; (2) consensus on agenda, procedures, and effectiveness; (3) representativeness and inclusiveness; (4) deliberation; (5) capability and social learning; (6) decision responsiveness; and (7) transparency and enhancement of trust.

The Co-Intelligence Institute (2008) has presented another mid-level set of principles to inform practice. They are called the Principles to Nurture Wise Democratic Process and Collective Intelligence in Public Participation. They consist of the following: (1) include all relevant perspectives; (2) empower the people's engagement; (3) invoke multiple forms of knowing; (4) ensure high-quality dialogue; (5) establish ongoing participatory processes; and (6) use positions and proposals as grist and help people feel fully heard.

A recent compilation of additional guiding principles (Shulha et al., 2016), discussed earlier, focuses on stakeholder involvement approaches. Together, these are important generic principles that provide an overarching form of guidance.

Macro- and midlevel principles, although useful, have limited value or applicability on the microlevel of analysis. For example, negotiating a balance of power is appropriate and useful for participatory evaluation; however, it is typically already determined in collaborative evaluation (the evaluator retains most of the power) and empowerment evaluation (the community assumes most of the power). Similarly, empowerment evaluation highlights *community control*, as compared with a *partnership* in participatory evaluation or *involvement* in a collaborative evaluation.

Microlevel Principles

Principles associated with individual evaluation approaches might be viewed as the microlevel of analysis, which focuses on principles needed for the actual implementation of specific approaches on a daily basis. For example, empathy, social support, and trust apply to all approaches, but they are particularly important principles to guide collaborative evaluation because of the need to bridge, or compensate for, the inherent distance or power differential between the evaluator and the stakeholders. Everyone sharing control of the evaluation, negotiating the balance of power, and jointly setting out objectives matches participatory evaluation perfectly, because of the commitment to shared power. These principles help ensure that the spirit of the approach is adhered to during the evaluation. Community ownership, capacity building, and accountability capture the balance of power purposely weighted toward the community or program staff member side of the scale, reinforcing the appropriate locus of control and responsibility for results in empowerment evaluation.

The macro-, mid-, and microlevels of analysis offer a useful heuristic to view and apply the principles (see Table 11.1). These principles were

TABLE 11.1. Macro-, Mid-, and Microlevel Principles

Macrolevel (examples)

American Evaluation Association's Guiding Principles for Evaluation
systematic inquiry, competence, integrity/honesty, respect for people,
and responsibility for general and public welfare

Australasian Evaluation Society
commissioning and preparing for an evaluation, conducting an evaluation,
and reporting the results of an evaluation

Canadian Evaluation Society
competence, integrity, and accountability

Caribbean Evaluators International
ethical, excellence, professionalism, inclusiveness, and transparency

South African Monitoring and Evaluation Association
high-quality intellectual, ethical, and professional standards

Midlevel (examples)

CPE-TIG generated lists of principles
accountability, capacity building, community knowledge, community ownership,
competence, democratic participation, empathy, empowerment, evaluation use,
evidence-based strategies, improvement, organizational learning, self-determination,
social justice, social support, sustainability, and trust

CPE-TIG survey results
70–92% in agreement—capacity building, improvement, evaluation use, trust,
organizational learning, community knowledge, accountability, empathy, evidence-
based practices, and sustainability

45–66% in agreement—social justice, democratic participation, community
ownership, competence, empowerment, social support, and self-determination

Additional CPE-TIG survey results
equity, accessibility, results, culturally competent, integrity, fairness, standards,
diversity, open communication, resilience, ethics, transformative, transparency,
respect, accuracy, collaborative, humility, courage, engagement, and humor

Additional stakeholder-involvement approaches to evaluation survey results
clarify motivation for collaboration, foster meaningful relationships, develop a shared
understanding of the program, promote appropriate participatory processes, monitor
and respond to resource availability, monitor evaluation progress and quality, promote
evaluative thinking, and follow through to realize use

(continued)

TABLE 11.1. *(continued)*		
Microlevel (examples)		
Collaborative evaluation	*Participatory evaluation*	*Empowerment evaluation*
• Development • Empathy • Empowerment • Involvement • Qualification • Social support • Trust	• Participant focus and ownership • Negotiation and balance of power • Learning • Flexibility • Focus on action planning • Sharing control • Objectives set jointly • Work out difficulties together • Awareness raising	• Improvement • Community ownership • Inclusion • Democratic participation • Social justice • Community knowledge • Evidence-based strategies • Capacity building • Organizational learning • Accountability

developed independently, for different purposes, and for varying circumstances and contexts. Therefore, it is not surprising that the lines are not precisely drawn between them. However, they already provide invaluable macro-, mid-, and microlevel guidance and direction for stakeholder involvement approaches to evaluation.

The next step is to apply a principles-focused evaluation approach (using GUIDE[4] criteria) to further refine these stakeholder involvement approaches to evaluation principles (Patton, 2018). As Patton (2018) explains, "Evaluating adherence to evaluation principles is a source of our professional accountability and, indeed, stature as a principles-based profession. Being a principles-based profession improves and guides further development of our evaluation practices" (p. 306).

Shared Methods and Skills

In addition to principles, collaborative, participatory, and empowerment evaluators use many of the same methods in practice.[5] This is in part because the approaches are more about a systematic way of thinking and practicing evaluation than they are about the use of particular methods. For example, they all use qualitative and quantitative methods.

Typical methods used across approaches include literature searches, data collection (e.g., surveys, interviews, observations, storytelling [concerning storytelling in evaluation, see Krueger, 2012; McClintock, 2004], photovoice [for a presentation about photovoice, see Daw, 2011], and fieldwork), and analysis. Tools include self-rating exercises, logic models, dialogues, document reviews, and dashboards to monitor performance. Equipment includes computers, smart phones with cameras, digital recorders, and poster boards to record group exchanges. Qualitative data analysis software includes NVivo, Atlas.ti, and HyperResearch. Quantitative software includes Excel, SAS, and SPSS. Web-based tools include video conferencing and e-mail to facilitate communication (e.g., Zoom, Google Hangout, Skype, and gmail). Online surveys are used to take the pulse of the group, program, and community (e.g., SurveyMonkey and Google Forms). Collaborative document, spreadsheet, and slide-sharing software are used to encourage participation, build rapport, and enhance quality. Blogging, social media, and infographics/data visualization are used to report on progress, problems, and accomplishments.

Facilitation skills are required in all stakeholder involvement approaches to evaluation, given the diversity of most groups and the vested interests entrenched in program and community dynamics. Research and management skills are also an absolute requirement. In addition, cultural sensitivity and competence are needed and a nonjudgmental approach is highly valued. Furthermore, interpersonal communication skills, verbal and written skills, and a concern and deep respect for other people are required. Fundamentally, one of the most important skills among these approaches is the ability to share and/or relinquish power (to some degree).

CONCLUSION

Collaborative, participatory, and empowerment evaluation approaches have much in common. They are all stakeholder involvement approaches to evaluation. In addition, they share common guiding principles and practices, including methods. They require many of the same skill sets. Moreover, all are appropriate for culturally diverse contexts and populations. They give voice to previously marginalized populations. Collaborative, participatory, and empowerment evaluation are all democratic, inclusive, and transparent in style and substance. The principles and practices discussed in this chapter are woven into the fabric of collaborative, participatory, and empowerment evaluation approaches, producing a rich tapestry of stakeholder involvement approaches to evaluation.

Together collaborative, participatory, and empowerment evaluation represent a tremendous force for social well-being and equity.

NOTES

1. The participatory evaluation box is a compilation of guiding principles developed by independent individuals and agencies conducting participatory evaluations because there is no unifying or agreed-upon set of guiding principles for participatory evaluation.

2. There is much work ahead concerning the definition of principles. For example, collaborative evaluation is guided by empowerment. However, this conception of empowerment (although focused on helping people feel more empowered) is radically different from empowerment as manifested by empowerment evaluation practices. The former is guided by the evaluator and thus involves a more limited conception of empowerment, while the later places the evaluation in the community's hands, resulting in a completely different level of empowerment in practice.

3. Empowerment and self-determination are similar. However, the group decided to keep both in the list because they viewed them as separate concepts. One way to highlight the difference is that *self-determination skills* are used to acquire a sense of *empowerment* or control.

4. GUIDE refers to a specific set of criteria used to evaluate the effectiveness of a principle. Specifically, "A high-quality principle (1) provides guidance, (2) is useful, (3) inspires, (4) supports ongoing development and adaptation, and (5) is evaluable" (Patton, 2018, p. 36).

5. There are differences across approaches concerning who are the primary users of the methods (e.g., evaluator, community member, and/or both).

APPENDIX 11.1. Commonalities across Evaluation Approaches

	Collaborative evaluation	Participatory evaluation	Empowerment evaluation
Explicit	Involvement	Involvement	Involvement (Inclusion)
	Participant focus	Participant focus	Participant focus
	Capacity building (development)	Capacity building (participant focus and learning)	Capacity building
	Community knowledge	Community knowledge	Community knowledge
	Learning	Learning	Learning
	Improvement	Improvement	Improvement
	Social justice (potentially)	Social justice (potentially)	Social justice
	Empowerment (potentially)	Empowerment (potentially)	Empowerment
Implicit	Trust	Trust	Trust
	Ownership	Ownership	Ownership
	Qualifications	Qualifications	Qualifications
	Empathy/sensitivity	Empathy/sensitivity	Empathy/sensitivity
	Democratic participation	Democratic participation	Democratic participation
	Evidence-based strategies (potentially)	Evidence-based strategies (potentially)	Evidence-based strategies
	Organizational learning (potentially)	Organizational learning (potentially)	Organizational learning
	Accountability	Accountability (potentially)	Accountability
	Flexibility	Flexibility	Flexibility

CHAPTER 12

Conclusion

Highlighting the Present
and Looking to the Future

David M. Fetterman, Liliana Rodríguez-Campos,
Abraham Wandersman, Rita Goldfarb O'Sullivan,
and Ann P. Zukoski

Stakeholder involvement approaches to evaluation are powerful responses to pressing social problems. These approaches appreciate community knowledge and values. They support local control to varying degrees. In addition, they contribute to program improvement, building capacity, and producing results. Collaborative, participatory, and empowerment evaluations are often more credible than traditional approaches in serving marginalized communities. They cultivate a sense of ownership, which increases the probability of use and programmatic sustainability.

Stakeholder involvement approaches to evaluation are conducted worldwide. However, they are not monolithic. There are distinctive differences among approaches, particularly concerning the role of the evaluator. While we acknowledge the differences between approaches, we also see many similarities. For example, they share many principles, values, methods, and skills. Although each approach can and often should be applied by itself, the field is prepared for a new era of stakeholder involvement approaches to evaluation experimentation. One promising path is combining approaches in the same initiative, depending on the circumstances, purpose, funding, and context.

INTERNATIONAL EVALUATIONS

Although some of the most widely documented examples of stakeholder involvement approaches to evaluation are based on work conducted in the United States (as highlighted in the case examples in this book), stakeholder involvement approaches are being conducted throughout the world (Figure 12.1). For example, collaborative evaluations have been used in a wide variety of settings and countries including a market survey of wholesalers in southern Sudan (O'Sullivan & O'Sullivan, 2012; O'Sullivan & Rodríguez-Campos, 2012); a training program to support organizational competitiveness in the Caribbean (Walker-Egea, 2015); a finance and banking corporation in the Asian-Pacific region (Nguyen & Pham, 2015); an intervention in family treatment in Mexico (López Beltrám, 2011); and as a mechanism for improving evaluation of classroom learning in Colombia (Collazos, Ochoa, & Mendoza, 2007).

Participatory evaluations are also conducted throughout the world. The range of problems addressed is extensive. For example, participatory evaluation has been used to help assess popular theater approaches to HIV/AIDS in Tanzania (Bagamoyo College of Arts, Tanzania Theatre Centre, Mabala, & Allen, 2002) and teacher in-service training programs in India (Cousins & RMSA Evaluation Team, 2015). A participatory evaluation approach was also used to assess poverty alleviation

FIGURE 12.1. Dr. Rodríguez-Campos providing collaborative evaluation training at the International Center of Economic Policy for Sustainable Development in Costa Rica, 2013.

projects in Africa (Gariba, 1998) and a project in the Philippines focused on a vegetable home gardens project designed to establish food security (Campilan, Prain, & Bagalanon, 1999). Additional participatory evaluations have been conducted in agriculturally related projects in Indonesia (Asmunati, 1999) and Nepal (Ghimire & Dhital, 1998). Participatory evaluations have also been conducted in Latin America and the Caribbean (Rice & Franceschini, 2007).

Empowerment evaluation initiatives are being conducted in over 16 countries, ranging from high-tech companies in the United States, like Google (Ravitz & Fetterman, 2016) and Hewlett-Packard (Fetterman, 2013c), to squatter settlements and townships in South Africa (Fetterman, 2001a). Peruvian women are using empowerment evaluation to improve their crafts and sell them on the Internet, thereby bypassing the middle person who previously consumed a disproportionate amount of the profit (Sastre-Merino et al., 2015). Australian teachers (and teachers in other countries) are using empowerment evaluation to improve instruction and student learning (Clinton & Hattie, 2015). Empowerment evaluation is also being used in Mexico to help marginalized rural indigenous communities (Figueroa, 2007). They are using GIS to help identify and share local community resources in order to build economically sustainable communities. The range of programs and projects using stakeholder involvement approaches is enormous and the scope is literally global.

DIFFERENCES BETWEEN APPROACHES

It must be acknowledged that there are clear differences between the most commonly used approaches. This collection has highlighted the differences and essential features between the three approaches discussed here, and has provided multiple case examples of each approach. For example, collaborative evaluators are *in charge* of an evaluation, but they create an ongoing engagement between themselves and stakeholders; participatory evaluators *jointly share* control of the evaluation; and empowerment evaluators view *program staff members, program participants, and community members as themselves in control* of the evaluation. These role differences have implications for the conduct of the evaluation and the benefits derived from them. Differentiating and clarifying approaches[1] help evaluators (and community members and funders) select the most appropriate stakeholder involvement approach, given the purpose, context, setting, and goals.

An Illustration

A simple illustration highlights the distinctive difference between the three evaluation approaches and why it is important to select the most appropriate approach for the program or task at hand. A school administrator operating a program for students who had dropped out of the regular school system requested an evaluation to improve its services. The school administrator recognized the need for an approach that respected the school community. She also understood that the approach selected had to anticipate and invite community involvement throughout the process. She distributed a request for proposals and received three stakeholder involvement approaches to evaluation proposals.

The first one was a *collaborative* evaluation proposal. The proposal explained how the evaluator would be *in charge* of the evaluation. School community members would be *consulted* and involved at every step (to the extent of their ability and availability) in the evaluation. The evaluator would conduct interviews and focus groups with students, teachers, administrators, and parents. In addition, the evaluator would ask all of them to help design the evaluation and conduct parts of it alongside the evaluator. However, the evaluator would be responsible for the majority of the data collection, analysis, and reporting (including recommendations).

The second proposal adopted a *participatory* evaluation approach. It explained how the evaluation would be *shared*. The evaluators would ask students, teachers, administrators, and parents to *participate* in the process of designing the evaluation, collecting data, doing analysis, and reporting findings and recommendations. Initially, participatory evaluators might provide leadership and training, but responsibility for the evaluation (including decision making) would be shared through most of the evaluation.

The third proposal was an *empowerment evaluation* submission. It explained how the students, teachers, administrators, and parents were *in charge* of the evaluation. The proposal described the roles and responsibilities of the school personnel. It also described the training and support they would receive throughout the evaluation. The empowerment evaluator, in particular, would serve as a coach, critical friend, and facilitator guiding the evaluation. The school community, however, would be responsible for collecting data, doing the analysis, and reporting, once again with the guidance and assistance of the empowerment evaluator.

This simple example highlights the different roles for the evaluator. Moreover, it describes the level of stakeholder involvement expected in each approach. The selection of any given approach has implications for everyone's time, resources, capacity, and goals. The scope and complexity of the initiative also needs to be taken into consideration. A complex initiative with limited funding may preclude extensive participation and capacity building. However, the same complex evaluation may require extensive stakeholder involvement if the goal is capacity building and sustainability, and the funding permits such interaction. The timeline as well as the resources devoted to both capacity building and program implementation need to be a part of, in this example, the proposal selection equation. In any case, all of the stakeholder involvement approaches value stakeholders' views and expect them to be a part of the evaluation.

SIMILARITIES AMONG APPROACHES

Although stakeholder involvement approaches to evaluation have clear distinctions between them (as highlighted by the previous example), they have more in common than they do in the differences that define them. For example, there are many guiding principles for stakeholder involvement approaches to evaluation in common. Specifically, they share the following principles: involvement, participant focus, capacity building, valuing community knowledge, learning, and improvement. The long list of additional guiding principles can be made more manageable and useful by organizing them according to macrolevel, midlevel, and microlevels of analysis. Macrolevel principles are the most broad and overarching (such as the AEA's Guiding Principles), midlevel principles focus on a subset of the larger population (such as stakeholder involvement approaches), and microlevel principles are most relevant and useful when applying a specific stakeholder involvement approach to evaluation—for example, collaborative, participatory, or empowerment evaluation. These evaluation approaches also rely on the same methods and skills. They also all require the ability to share and/or relinquish some degree of power.

COMBINING APPROACHES

Once the evaluator, staff, community members, and the funder are familiar with the similarities and differences across stakeholder involvement approaches to evaluation, consideration should be given to experimenting with the approaches by combining them. The advantage to be gained is substantial where and when a combination is merited. For example, the W. K. Kellogg Foundation's board of trustees approved the use of empowerment evaluation as part of its evaluation repertoire in 2013 (Fetterman, Wandersman, & Kaftarian, 2015). Dr. Fetterman was invited to facilitate empowerment evaluation exercises in Battle Creek, Michigan, and in Mexico City. The exercises were designed to help grantees in Mexico monitor and assess their place-based initiatives, building on their own efforts in their microregions (Figure 12.2).

The groups developed self-monitoring evaluation dashboards with the assistance of an empowerment evaluator, Oscar Figueroa, and the program officers, Paco Martinez, Gustavo Maldonado, and Juan Antonio Flores. The dashboards compared annual goals and quarterly milestones with actual performance throughout the year. The dashboards included plans for evaluating 100 schools concerning indigenous education (see Figure 12.3); adding women to community-based boards to raise consciousness about the role of women politically, economically, and socially; and improving water usage for human consumption and irrigation. The approach resonated with the grantees and complemented their own efforts, producing desired results or outcomes.

FIGURE 12.2. Dr. Fetterman and a Latin American and Caribbean group engaged in a W. K. Kellogg Foundation–sponsored empowerment discussion.

Not all grantees wanted or needed to conduct the evaluation themselves. Some W. K. Kellogg Foundation groups wanted their work to be monitored and assessed, but lacked the time for or interest in conducting the evaluation themselves. Moreover, their evaluation needs were specific, the project duration was short, and the deadlines were less flexible. For those groups, a collaborative evaluation approach was adopted. It worked in parallel with an empowerment evaluation, without difficulty or conflict. The collaborative evaluation group remained in charge of that portion of the evaluation, but consulted staff and grantees extensively. They also facilitated focus groups and brainstorming exercises to collect data from grantees and the community. The collaborative evaluation team conducted the analysis and produced the report. It provided these W. K. Kellogg Foundation groups with the information needed to respond to specific operational questions and pursue their work without the burden associated with conducting the evaluation themselves. It was a learning opportunity, but more limited in scope and depth. Although it minimally contributed to self-determination or building evaluation capacity in the community, it was expedient and all that was needed for the focused task at the time. The collaborative evaluation group and empowerment evaluation groups consulted with each other on a regular

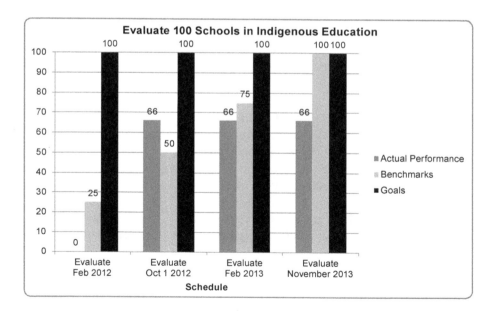

FIGURE 12.3. Evaluation monitoring dashboard—highlighting an evaluation of indigenous education in Mexico.

and ongoing basis to learn from each other and reinforce each other's efforts.

There will continue to be many evaluations requiring the services of only one stakeholder involvement approach to evaluation. Increasingly, however, programs and communities may find that one approach may not be sufficient to meet their needs. This is just an emerging reality to meet the needs of people living in complex systems. There are an extraordinary number of conceivable combinations to meet these needs, depending on the purpose, scope, deadline, and funding associated with the initiative. These hybrid stakeholder involvement approaches to evaluation designs are limited only by the imagination of the groups creating them (including evaluators, staff, community members, and funders), the principles and methodological standards guiding them, and the resources available.

SUMMARY THOUGHTS AND REFLECTIONS

This collection symbolizes a commitment to clarity and it represents one contribution to improve evaluation practice. Defining terms, explaining differences, and highlighting similarities contribute to knowledge and understanding. Providing greater conceptual clarity and methodological rigor is an essential part of scientific inquiry.

This book provides a solid conceptual foundation for stakeholder involvement approaches to evaluation. It highlights the essential features of these approaches to evaluation, methodological similarities, and guiding principles in common. Case examples demonstrate how each approach is implemented. The examples throughout the book also shed light on how stakeholder involvement approaches to evaluation can contribute to the task of addressing pressing social concerns.

This collection is not, however, designed to be exhaustive in terms of the range of stakeholder involvement approaches or the issues associated with the application of these approaches. The primary practical contribution of this book is helping evaluators, staff members, community members, and funders select the most appropriate (or combination of appropriate) stakeholder involvement approaches to evaluation. Guiding principles have been discussed in part because they are a common thread woven throughout stakeholder involvement approaches to evaluation. In addition, they further enhance the quality of each approach.

Tremendous strides have been made in stakeholder involvement approaches to evaluation over the last couple of decades, building a strong conceptual foundation, enhancing conceptual clarity, and maintaining methodological rigor. One of the next key steps is to explore and experiment with various combinations of stakeholder involvement approaches to evaluation by adhering to their principles and standards, but pushing the edges of the envelope.

Stakeholder involvement approaches are a part of the intellectual landscape of evaluation. They have played a significant role in enhancing use and helping people accomplish their goals. It is an evolving science and will continue to benefit from our continued dialogue, critique, and exchange.

NOTE

1. In addition to the long list of scholars currently requesting greater clarity between stakeholder involvement approaches to evaluation, participatory evaluation scholars have been recommending greater clarity for almost a decade. According to Campilan (2000, p. 35), given the multiple meanings associated with evaluation, participation, and participatory evaluation, there is a need to monitor the language being used in an atmosphere of open-mindedness and mutual respect. This is essential for participatory evaluators to better communicate and learn from each other.

References

Abracen, J., & Looman, J. (2015). *Treatment of high risk sexual offenders: An integrated approach*. New York: Wiley-Blackwell.

Alkin, M. (2017). When is a theory a theory?: A case example. *Evaluation and Program Planning, 63*, 141–142.

American Diabetes Association. (2012.) Statistics about diabetes. Retrieved from *www.diabetes.org/diabetes-basics/statistics*.

American Evaluation Association. (2004). American Evaluation Association Guiding Principles for Evaluators. Retrieved from *www.eval.org/p/cm/ld/fid=51*.

Argyris, C., & Schön, D. A. (1978). *Organizational learning: A theory of action perspective*. Reading, MA: Addison-Wesley.

Arnold, M. E. (2006). Developing evaluation capacity in extension 4-H field faculty: A framework for success. *American Journal of Evaluation, 27*, 257–269.

Asmunati, R. (1999). Participatory monitoring and evaluation of the sweet potato ICM farmer field schools in Indonesia. *UPWARD Fieldnotes, 6*(1), 15–17.

Bagamoyo College of Arts, Tanzania Theatre Centre, Mabala, R., & Allen, K. B. (2002). Participatory action research on HIV/AIDS through a popular theatre approach in Tanzania. *Evaluation and Programme Planning, 25*, 333–339.

Bandura, A. (1977). Self-efficacy: Toward a unifying theory of behavioral change. *Psychological Review, 84*(2), 191–215.

Black, M. C., Basile, K. C., Breiding, M. J., Smith, S. G., Walters, M. L., Merrick, M. T., et al. (2011). *The National Intimate Partner and Sexual Violence Survey (NISVS): 2010 Summary Report*. Atlanta, GA: National Center for Injury Prevention and Control, Centers for Disease Control and Prevention.

Bledsoe, K. L., & Graham, J. A. (2005). The use of multiple evaluation approaches in program evaluation. *American Journal of Evaluation, 26*, 302–319.

Brown, J., Issaacs, D., & the World Café Community. (2008). *The World Café: Shaping our futures through conversations that matter*. San Francisco: Berrett-Koehler.

Campilan, D. (2000, December). *Participatory evaluation of participatory research.* Paper presented at the forum Evaluation of International Cooperation Projects: Centering on Development of Human Resources in the Field of Agriculture, International Potato Center, Nagoya, Japan. Retrieved from *http://ir.nul.nagoya-u.ac.jp/jspui/bitstream/2237/8890/1/39-56.pdf.*

Campilan, D., Prain, G., & Bagalanon, C. (1999). Evaluation from the inside: Participatory evaluation of agricultural research in the Philippines. *Knowledge and Policy, 11*(4), 114–131.

Canadian International Development Agency. (2001). How to perform evaluations: Participatory evaluations. Retrieved from *www.oecd.org/derec/Canada/35135226.pdf.*

Centers for Disease Control and Prevention. (2008). *STD surveillance report, 2006.* Atlanta, GA: U.S. Department of Health and Human Services.

Centers for Disease Control and Prevention. (n.d.). HIV/AIDS surveillance—adolescents and young adults. Retrieved from *https://www.cdc.gov/hiv/pdf/statistics_surveillance_Adolescents.pdf.*

Chambers, R. (2009). Making the poor count: Using participatory options for impact evaluation. In R. Chambers, D. Karlan, M. Ravallion, & P. Rogers (Eds.), *Designing impact evaluations: Different perspectives.* New Delhi, India: International Initiative for Impact Evaluation. Retrieved from *www.3ieimpact.org/admin/pdfs_papers/50.pdf.*

Chinman, M., Acosta, J., Ebener, P., Sigel, C., & Keith, J. (2016). *Getting to Outcomes: Guide for teen pregnancy prevention.* Santa Monica, CA: RAND. Retrieved from *https://www.rand.org/content/dam/rand/pubs/tools/TL100/TL199/RAND_TL199.pdf.*

Chinman, M., Hunter, S. B., Ebener, P., Paddock, S. M., Stillman, L., Imm, P., et al. (2008). The Getting To Outcomes demonstration and evaluation: An illustration of the prevention support system. *American Journal of Community Psychology, 41*(3–4), 206–224.

Chinman, M., Imm, P., & Wandersman, A. (2004). *Getting To Outcomes: Promoting accountability through methods and tools for planning, implementation, and evaluation.* Santa Monica, CA: RAND Corporation. Retrieved from *www.rand.org/pubs/technical_reports/TR101.*

Chouinard, J. A., & Hopson, R. (2016). Toward a more critical exploration of culture in international development evaluation. *Canadian Journal for Program Evaluation, 30*(3), 248–276.

Clinton, J., & Hattie, J. (2015). Teachers as evaluators: An empowerment evaluation approach. In D. M. Fetterman, S. Kaftarian, & A. Wandersman (Eds.), *Empowerment evaluation: Knowledge and tools for self-assessment, evaluation capacity building, and accountability* (2nd ed., pp. 86–111). Thousand Oaks, CA: SAGE.

Co-Intelligence Institute. (2008). Principles of public participation: Principles to nurture wise democratic process and collective intelligence in public participation. Retrieved from *www.co-intelligence.org/CIPol_publicparticipation.html.*

Collazos, C., Ochoa, S., & Mendoza, J. (2007). Collaborative evaluation as a mechanism for improving evaluation of classroom learning [La evaluación colaborativa como mecanismo de mejora en los procesos de evaluación del aprendizaje en un aula de clase]. *Revista Ingeniería en Investigación, 27*(2), 1–7.

Committee on Early Childhood, Adoption, and Dependent Care. (2005). Quality early education and child care from birth to kindergarten. *Pediatrics, 115*, 187–191. Retrieved from *http://pediatrics.appublications.org/content/115/1/187.*

Cornwall, A. (2008). Unpacking "participation": Models, meanings and practices. *Community Development Journal, 43*(3), 269–283.

Cousins, J. B. (2005). Will the real empowerment evaluation please stand up?: A critical friend perspective. In D. M. Fetterman & A. Wandersman (Eds.), *Empowerment evaluation principles in practice* (pp. 183–208). New York: Guilford Press.

Cousins, J. B., & Chouinard, J. A. (2012). *Participatory evaluation up close: An integration of research based knowledge.* Charlotte, NC: Information Age.

Cousins, J. B., Donohue, J. J., & Bloom, G. A. (1996). Collaborative evaluation in North America: Evaluators' self-reported opinions, practices, and consequences. *Evaluation Practice, 17*(3), 207–226.

Cousins, J. B., & Earl, L. M. (1992). The case for participatory evaluation. *Educational Evaluation and Policy Analysis, 14*, 397–418.

Cousins, J. B., & Earl, L. M. (1995). Participatory evaluation: Enhancing evaluation use and organizational learning capacity. Retrieved from *www.hfrp.org/evaluation/the-evaluation-exchange/issue-archive/participatory   evaluation/participatory-evaluation-enhancing-evaluation-use-and-organizational-learning capacity.*

Cousins, J. B., & RMSA Evaluation Team. (2015, September). *Formative evaluation of RMSA teacher in-service training: Summary report.* New Delhi, India: RMSA-Technical Co-operation Agency.

Cousins, J. B., & Whitmore, E. (1998). Framing participatory evaluation. In E. Whitmore (Ed.), *Understanding and practicing participatory evaluation* (*New Directions for Evaluation, No. 80,* pp. 3–23). San Francisco: Jossey-Bass.

Cousins, J. B., Whitmore, E., & Shulha, L. (2013). Arguments for a common set of principles for collaborative inquiry in evaluation. *American Journal of Evaluation, 34,* 7–22.

Cousins, J. B., Whitmore, E., Shulha, L., al Hudib, H., & Gilbert, N. (2015, September). Principles to guide collaborative approaches to evaluation. Retrieved from *https://evaluationcanada.ca/sites/default/files/20170131_caebrochure_en.pdf.*

Crishna, B. (2006). Participatory evaluation (1): Sharing lessons from fieldwork in Asia. *Child Care, Health and Development, 33*(3), 217–223.

Daigneault, P., & Jacob, S. (2009). Toward accurate measurement of participation: Rethinking the conceptualization and operation of participatory evaluation. *American Journal of Evaluation, 30*(3), 330–348.

Datta, L. (2016, August 16). Book review of *Empowerment evaluation: Knowledge and tools for self-assessment, evaluation capacity building, and accountability. American Journal of Evaluation,* pp. 1–5.

Daw, M. (2011). See it our way: Participatory photography as a tool for advocacy. Retrieved from *www.photovoice.org/html/ppforadvocacy/ppforadvocacy.pdf.*

Donaldson, S. (2017). Empowerment evaluation: An approach that has literally altered the landscape of evaluation. *Evaluation and Program Planning, 63,* 136–137.

Donaldson, S. I., Patton, M. Q., Fetterman, D. M., & Scriven, M. (2010). The Claremont debates: The promise and pitfalls of utilization-focused and empowerment evaluation. *Journal of Multidisciplinary Evaluation, 6*(13), 15–57.

Endo, T., Joh, T., & Cao Yu, H. (2003). *Voices from the field: Health and evaluation leaders on multicultural evaluation.* Oakland, CA: Social Policy Research Associates, The California Endowment.

Fay, B. (1975). *Social theory and political practice.* London: Allen & Unwin.

Fetterman, D. M. (1994). Empowerment evaluation. *Evaluation Practice, 15*(1), 1–15.

Fetterman, D. M. (1997). Empowerment evaluation: A response to Patton and Scriven. *Evaluation Practice, 18*(3), 255–260.

Fetterman, D. M. (Ed.). (2001a). *Foundations of empowerment evaluation.* Thousand Oaks, CA: SAGE.

Fetterman, D. M. (2001b). The standards: Applying the standards to empowerment evaluation. In D. M. Fetterman (Ed.), *Foundations of empowerment evaluation* (pp. 87–99). Thousand Oaks, CA: SAGE.

Fetterman, D. M. (2005a). Empowerment evaluation: From digital divide to academic distress. In D. M. Fetterman & A. Wandersman (Eds.), *Empowerment evaluation principles in practice.* New York: Guilford Press.

Fetterman, D. M. (2005b). Empowerment evaluation principles in practice: Assessing levels of commitment. In D. M. Fetterman & A. Wandersman (Eds.), *Empowerment evaluation principles in practice* (pp. 42–72). New York: Guilford Press.

Fetterman, D. M. (2005c). In response to Drs. Patton and Scriven. *American Journal of Evaluation, 26*(3), 418–420.

Fetterman, D. M. (2009). Empowerment evaluation at the Stanford University School of Medicine: Using a critical friend to improve the clerkship experience. *Ensaio, 17*(63), 197–204.

Fetterman, D. M. (2012). Empowerment evaluation and accreditation case examples: California Institute of Integral Studies and Stanford University. In C. Secolsky & D. B. Denison (Eds.), *Handbook on measurement, assessment, and evaluation in higher education* (pp. 90–99). New York: Routledge.

Fetterman, D. M. (2013a). Empowerment evaluation: Learning to think like an evaluator. In M. C. Alkin (Ed.), *Evaluation roots* (3rd ed., pp. 304–322). Thousand Oaks, CA: SAGE.

Fetterman, D. M. (2013b). *Empowerment evaluation in the digital villages: Hewlett-Packard's $15 million race toward social justice.* Stanford, CA: Stanford University Press.

Fetterman, D. M. (2013c). *Infographics, data visualizations, and evaluation: Helping evaluators help themselves.* Washington, DC: American Evaluation Association.

Fetterman, D. M. (2015). Empowerment evaluation: Theories, principles, concepts, and steps. In D. M. Fetterman, S. Kaftarian, & A. Wandersman (Eds.), *Empowerment evaluation: Knowledge and tools for self-assessment, evaluation capacity building, and accountability* (2nd ed., pp. 20–42). Thousand Oaks, CA: SAGE.

Fetterman, D. M. (2017). Transformative empowerment evaluation and Freireian pedagogy: Alignment with an emancipatory tradition. In M. Q. Patton (Ed.), *Pedagogy of evaluation: Contributions of Paulo Freire to global evaluation thinking and practice (New Directions for Evaluation).* San Francisco: Jossey-Bass.

Fetterman, D. M., & Bowman, C. (2002). Experiential education and empowerment evaluation: Mars Rover educational program case example. *Journal of Experiential Education, 25*(2), 286–295.

Fetterman, D. M., Deitz, J., & Gesundheit, N. (2010). Empowerment evaluation: A collaborative approach to evaluating and transforming a medical school curriculum. *Academic Medicine, 85,* 813–820.

Fetterman, D. M., Delaney, L., Triana-Tremain, B., & Evans-Lee, M. (2015). Empowerment evaluation and evaluation capacity building in a 10-year tobacco prevention initiative. In D. M. Fetterman, S. J. Kaftarian, & A. Wandersman (Eds.), *Empowerment evaluation: Knowledge and tools for self-assessment, evaluation capacity building, and accountability* (2nd ed., pp. 295–314). Thousand Oaks, CA: SAGE.

Fetterman, D. M., Kaftarian, S., & Wandersman, A. (Eds.). (1996). *Empowerment evaluation: Knowledge and tools for self-assessment and accountability.* Thousand Oaks, CA: SAGE.

Fetterman, D. M., Kaftarian, S., & Wandersman, A. (Eds.). (2015). *Empowerment evaluation: Knowledge and tools for self-assessment, evaluation capacity building, and accountability* (2nd ed.). Thousand Oaks, CA: SAGE.

Fetterman, D. M., & Ravitz, J. (2017). Evaluation capacity building. In B. Frey (Ed.), *The SAGE encyclopedia of educational research, measurement, and evaluation.* Thousand Oaks, CA: SAGE.

Fetterman, D. M., Rodríquez-Campos, L., Wandersman, A., & O'Sullivan Goldfarb, R. G. (2014). Collaborative, participatory, and empowerment evaluation: Building a strong conceptual foundation for stakeholder involvement approaches to evaluation (a response to Cousins, Whitmore, and Shulha). *American Journal of Evaluation, 35*(1), 144–148.

Fetterman, D. M., & Wandersman, A. (Eds.). (2005). *Empowerment evaluation principles in practice.* New York: Guilford Press.

Fetterman, D. M., & Wandersman, A. (2007). Empowerment evaluation: Yesterday, today, and tomorrow. *American Journal of Evaluation, 28,* 179–198.

Fetterman, D. M., & Wandersman, A. (2010, November). *Empowerment evaluation essentials: Highlighting the essential features of empowerment evaluation.* Paper presented at the American Evaluation Association, San Antonio, TX.

Fetterman, D. M., & Wandersman, A. (Eds.). (2015). *Empowerment evaluation principles in practice.* New York: Guilford Press.

Fetterman, D. M., Wandersman, A., & Kaftarian, S. (2015a). Conclusion: Reflections on emergent themes and next steps revisited. In D. M. Fetterman, A. Wandersman, & S. Kaftarian (Eds.), *Empowerment evaluation: Knowledge and tools for self-assessment, evaluation capacity building, and accountability.* Thousand Oaks, CA: SAGE.

Fetterman, D. M., Wandersman, A., & Kaftarian, S. (2015b). Empowerment evaluation is a systematic way of thinking: A response to Michael Patton. *Evaluation and Program Planning, 52,* 10–14.

Figueroa, O. (2007). Guerrero, Mexico: Empowerment evaluation. Retrieved from *http://eevaluation.blogspot.com/2007/06/guerrero-mexico-empowerment-evaluation.html.*

Fischer, D., Imm, P., Chinman, M., & Wandersman, A. (2006). *Getting To Outcomes with developmental assets: Ten steps to measuring success in youth programs and communities.* Minneapolis, MN: Search.

Fisher, P. A., & Ball, T. J. (2005). Balancing empiricism and local cultural knowledge in the design of prevention research. *Journal of Urban Health: Bulletin of the New York Academy of Medicine, 82*(2, Suppl. 3), iii44–iii55.

Fredericks, K. A., & Durland, M. M. (2005). The historical evolution and basic concepts of social network analysis. In M. M. Durland & K. A. Fredericks (Eds.), *Social network analysis in program evaluation* (*New Directions for Evaluation, No. 107*, pp. 15–23). San Francisco: Jossey-Bass.

Gajda, R. (2004). Utilizing collaboration theory to evaluate strategic alliances. *American Journal of Evaluation, 25*, 65–77.

Gariba, S. (1998). Participatory impact assessment as a tool for change: Lessons from poverty alleviation projects in Africa. In E. T. Jackson & Y. Kassam (Eds.), *Knowledge shared: Participatory evaluation in development cooperation* (pp. 64–81). West Hartford, CT: Kumarian Press.

Ghimire, S. R., & Dhital, B. K. (1998). *Community approach to the management of bacterial wilt of potato in the hills of Nepal: A project terminal report* (Occasional Paper No. 98/1). Nepal: Lumle Agricultural Research Center.

Gibson, J. L., Ivancevich, J. M., & Donnelly, J. H. (2008). *Organizations: Behavior, structure, processes* (13th ed.). Burr Ridge, IL: McGraw-Hill.

Gloudemans, J., & Welsh, J. (2015). The model for collaborative evaluations in the education sector. In L. Rodríguez-Campos (Ed.), *Collaborative evaluations in practice: Insights from business, nonprofit, and education sectors.* Scottsdale, AZ: Information Age.

Green, B. L., Mulvey, L., Fisher, H. A., & Woratschek, F. (1996). Integrating program and evaluation values: A family support approach to program evaluation. *American Journal of Evaluation, 17*, 261–272.

Greene, J. C. (1997). Evaluation as advocacy. *American Journal of Evaluation, 18*(1), 25–35.

Guerere, C., & Hicks, T. (2015). The model for collaborative evaluations in the nonprofit sector. In L. Rodríguez-Campos (Ed.), *Collaborative evaluations in practice: Insights from business, nonprofit, and education sectors.* Scottsdale, AZ: Information Age.

Guijt, I. (2014). *Participatory approaches.* Methodological Briefs: Impact Evaluation 5, UNICEF Office of Research, Florence, Italy.

Guijt, I., & Gaventa, J. (1998). *Participatory monitoring and evaluation: Learning from change* (IDS Policy Briefing). Brighton, UK: University of Sussex. Retrieved from *www.ids.ac.uk/files/dmfile/PB12.pdf.*

Hall, J. N., Ahn, J., & Greene, J. C. (2011). Values engagement in evaluation: Ideas, illustrations, and implications. *American Journal of Evaluation, 33*(2), 195–207.

Hansen Kollock, D. A., Flage, L., Chazdon, S., Paine, N., & Higgins, L. (2012). Ripple effect mapping: A "radiant" way to capture program impacts. *Journal of Extension, 50*(5).

Hedberg, B. (1981). How organizations learn and unlearn. In P. C. Nystrom & W. H. Starbuck (Eds.), *Handbook of organizational design: Vol. 1. Adapting organizations to their environments.* Oxford, UK: Oxford University Press.

Huberman, M. (1987). Steps toward an integrated model of research utilization. *Knowledge: Creation, Diffusion, Utilization, 8*, 586–611.

Imm, P., Chinman, M., Wandersman, A., Rosenbloom, D., Guckenburg, S., & Leis,

R. (2006). *Preventing underage drinking: Using Getting To Outcomes with the SAMHSA strategic prevention framework to achieve results.* Santa Monica, CA: RAND Corporation.

Institute for Development Studies. (1998). Participatory monitoring and evaluation: Learning from change. Retrieved from *www.theinnovationcenter.org/files/Reflect-and-Improve_Toolkit.pdf.*

International Radiation Protection Association. (2012). *IRPA guiding principles for radiation protection professionals on stakeholder engagement.* Washington, DC: National Academy of Science.

Jackson, E. T., & Kassam, Y. (Eds.). (1998). *Knowledge shared: Participatory evaluation in development cooperation.* Bloomfield, CT: Kumarian Press.

Joint Committee on Standards for Educational Evaluation. (1994). *The program evaluation standards.* Thousand Oaks, CA: SAGE.

Joint Committee on Standards for Educational Evaluation. (2003). *The student evaluation standards: How to improve the evaluation of students.* Thousand Oaks, CA: SAGE.

Joint Committee on Standards for Educational Evaluation. (2009). *The personnel evaluation standards: How to assess systems for evaluating evaluators.* Thousand Oaks, CA: Corwin Press.

Joint Committee on Standards for Educational Evaluation. (2011). *The program evaluation standards: A guide for evaluators and evaluation users.* Thousand Oaks, CA: SAGE.

Jupp, D., Ali, S. I., & Barahona, C. (2010). Measuring empowerment?: Ask them. Quantifying qualitative outcomes from people's own analysis. *Sida Studies in Evaluation, 1,* 9.

Kaplan, F., & Bornet, C. (2014). A preparatory analysis of peer-grading for a digital humanities MOOC. Digital Humanities, Switzerland. Retrieved from *https://infoscience.epfl.ch/record/200911/files/DHArchive.pdf.*

Kilpatrick, D. G., Resnick, H. S., Ruggiero, K. J., Conoscenti, L. M., & McCauley, J. (2007). Drug-facilitated, incapacitated, and forcible rape: A national study (Document No. 219181). Available at *https://www.ncjrs.gov/pdffiles1/nij/grants/219181.pdf.*

King, J. A., Nielson, J. E., & Colby, J. (2004). Lessons for culturally competent evaluation from the study of a multicultural initiative. In M. Thompson-Robinson, R. Hopson, & S. SenGupta (Eds.), *In search of cultural competence in evaluation: Towards principles and practices (New Directions for Evaluation, No. 102,* pp. 67–79). San Francisco: Jossey-Bass.

Kirby, D. (2007). Sex and HIV programs: Their impact on sexual behaviors of young people throughout the world. *Journal of Adolescent Health, 40,* 206–217.

Kohler, P. K., Manhart, L. E., & Lafferty, W. I. (2008). Abstinence-only and comprehensive sex education and the initiation of sexual activity and teen pregnancy. *Journal of Adolescent Health, 42*(4), 344–351.

Krueger, R. A. (2012). Storytelling. Retrieved from *www.tc.umn.edu/~rkrueger/story.html.*

Kushner, S. (2000). *Personalizing evaluation.* London: SAGE.

Langhout, R., & Fernandez, J. (2015). Empowerment evaluation conducted by fourth and fifth grade students. In D. M. Fetterman, S. Kaftarian, & A. Wandersman (Eds.), *Empowerment evaluation: Knowledge and tools for self-assessment, evaluation capacity building, and accountability.* Thousand Oaks, CA: SAGE.

López-Beltrám, I. (2011). Collaborative evaluation as intervention in the family treatment: Case study [Evaluación colaborativa como intervención en el tratamiento familiar: Estudio de caso]. *Revista de Psicología GEPU, 2*(1), 164–180.

Love, A. J., & Russon, C. (2000). Building a worldwide evaluation community: Past, present, and future. *Evaluation and Program Planning, 23,* 449–459.

Martz, W. (2015). The model for collaborative evaluations in the business sector. In L. Rodríguez-Campos (Ed.), *Collaborative evaluations in practice: Insights from business, nonprofit, and education sectors.* Scottsdale, AZ: Information Age.

Mathisen, W. C. (1990). The problem solving community: A valuable alternative to disciplinary communities? *Knowledge: Creation, Diffusion, Utilization, 11,* 410–427.

Mattox, T., Hunter, S. B., Kilburn, M. R., & Wiseman, S. H. (2013). Getting to outcomes for home visiting: How to plan, implement, and evaluate a program in your community to support parents and their young children. Santa Monica, CA: RAND Corporation. Retrieved from *www.rand.org/pubs/tools/TL114.html.*

McClintock, C. (2004). Using narrative options to link program evaluation and organization development. *Evaluation Exchange, 9*(4). Retrieved from *www.hfrp.org/evaluation/the-evaluation-exchange/issue-archive/reflecting-on-the-past-and-future-of-evaluation/using-narrative-methods-to-link-program-evaluation-and-organization-development.*

Mercier, C. (1997). Participation in stakeholder-based evaluation: A case study. *Evaluation and Program Planning, 20*(4), 467–475.

Miller, R., & Campbell, R. (2006). Taking stock of empowerment evaluation: An empirical review. *American Journal of Evaluation, 27,* 296–319.

Morabito, S. M. (2002). Evaluator roles and strategies for expanding evaluation process influence. *American Journal of Evaluation, 23,* 321–330.

Nguyen, D., & Pham, T. (2015). *Utilizing collaborative evaluation in a finance and banking corporation.* In L. Rodríguez-Campos (Ed.), *Collaborative evaluations in practice: Insights from business, education, and nonprofit sectors.* Scottsdale, AZ: Information Age.

O'Sullivan, J. M., & O'Sullivan, R. G. (2012). Collaborative evaluation and market research converge: An innovative model agricultural development program evaluation in Southern Sudan. *Evaluation and Program Planning, 35*(4), 535–539.

O'Sullivan, R. G. (2004). *Practicing evaluation: A collaborative approach.* Thousand Oaks, CA: SAGE.

O'Sullivan, R. G. (2014). *EvAP Evaluation Institute training manual.* Chapel Hill, NC: Evaluation, Assessment and Policy Connections (EvAP), School of Education, University of North Carolina at Chapel Hill.

O'Sullivan, R. G., & Rodríguez-Campos, L. (2012). Collaborative evaluations: Theory and practice [Special Section]. *Journal of Evaluation and Program Planning, 35*(4), 517.

Patton, M. Q. (1997a). Toward distinguishing empowerment evaluation and placing it in a larger context. *American Journal of Evaluation, 18,* 147–163.

Patton, M. Q. (1997b). *Utilization-focused evaluation* (3rd ed.). Thousand Oaks, CA: SAGE.

Patton, M. Q. (2005). Toward distinguishing empowerment evaluation and placing it in a larger context: Take two. *American Journal of Evaluation, 26,* 408–414.

Patton, M. Q. (2015). Book review of *Empowerment evaluation: Knowledge and tools for self-assessment, evaluation capacity building, and accountability* (2nd ed.) (D. M. Fetterman, S. J. Kaftarian, & A. Wandersman, Eds.). *Evaluation and Program Planning, 52,* 15–18.

Patton, M. Q. (2017). Empowerment evaluation: Exemplary is its openness to dialogue, reflective practice, and process use. *Evaluation and Program Planning, 63,* 139–140.

Patton, M. Q. (2018). *Principles-focused evaluation: The GUIDE.* New York: Guilford Press.

Petts, J., & Leach, B. (2000). *Evaluating methods for public participation: A literature review* (R&D Technical Report No. E135). Bristol, UK: Environment Agency.

Preskill, H., & Torres, R. (1999). *Evaluative inquiry for learning in organizations.* Thousand Oaks, CA: SAGE.

Ravitz, J., & Fetterman, D. M. (2016). On using the power of rubrics and technology for empowerment evaluation at Google and beyond. Retrieved from *http://aea365.org/blog/?s=ravitz+and+fetterman&submit=Go.*

Ravitz, J., & Hoadley, C. (2005). Supporting change and scholarship through systematic review of online educational resources in professional development settings. *British Journal of Educational Technology, 36*(6), 957–974. Retrieved from *http://academia.edu/1139425.*

Rice, M., & Franceschini, M. C. (2007). Lessons learned from the application of a participatory evaluation methodology to healthy municipalities, cities, and communities initiatives in selected countries of the Americas. *Promotion and Education, 14*(2), 68–73.

Rodríguez-Campos, L. (2005). *Collaborative evaluations: A step-by-step model for the evaluator.* Tamarac, FL: Llumina Press.

Rodríguez-Campos, L. (2008). *Evaluaciones colaborativas: Un modelo paso a paso para el evaluador* [Collaborative evaluations: A step-by-step model for the evaluator]. Tamarac, FL: Llumina Press.

Rodríguez-Campos, L. (2012a). Advances in collaborative evaluations. *Journal of Evaluation and Program Planning, 35*(4), 523–528.

Rodríguez-Campos, L. (2012b). Stakeholder involvement in evaluation: Three decades of the *American Journal of Evaluation. Journal of MultiDisciplinary Evaluation, 8*(17), 57–79.

Rodríguez-Campos, L. (Ed.). (2015). *Collaborative evaluations in practice: Insights from business, nonprofit, and education sectors.* Scottsdale, AZ: Information Age.

Rodríguez-Campos, L., & O'Sullivan, R. (2010, November). *Collaborative evaluation essentials: Highlighting the essential features of collaborative evaluation.* Paper presented at the American Evaluation Association Conference, San Antonio, TX.

Rodríguez-Campos, L., & Rincones-Gómez, R. (2013). *Collaborative evaluations: Step-by-step* (2nd ed.). Stanford, CA: Stanford University Press.

Rodríguez-Campos, L., & Rincones-Gómez, R. (2017). Collaborative evaluations. In B. Frey (Ed.), *The SAGE encyclopedia of educational research, measurement, and evaluation*. Thousand Oaks, CA: SAGE.

Rogers, C. R. (1969). *Freedom to learn*. Columbus, OH: Merrill.

Ryan, K., Greene, J., Lincoln, Y., Mathison, S., & Mertens, D. M. (1998). Advantages and challenges of using inclusive evaluation approaches in evaluation practice. *American Journal of Evaluation, 19*, 101–122.

Sabo Flores, K. (Ed.). (2003). *Youth participatory evaluation: A field in the making* (*New Directions in Evaluation, No. 98*). San Francisco: Jossey-Bass.

Sabo Flores, S. (2007). *Youth participatory evaluation: Strategies for engaging young people in evaluation*. San Francisco: Jossey-Bass.

Sanders, J. (2005). Foreword. In L. Rodríguez-Campos (Ed.), *Collaborative evaluations: A step-by-step model for the evaluator*. Tamarac, FL: Llumina Press.

Sastre-Merino, S., Vidueira, P., Díaz-Puente, J. M., & Fernandez-Moral, E. (2015). Capacity building through empowerment evaluation: An Aymara women artisans organization in Puno, Peru. In D. M. Fetterman, S. Kaftarian, & A. Wandersman (Eds.), *Empowerment evaluation: Knowledge and tools for self-assessment, evaluation capacity building, and accountability*. Thousand Oaks, CA: SAGE.

Schwandt, T. A. (1997). The landscape of values in evaluation: Charted terrain and unexplored territory. In D. J. Rog & D. Fournier (Eds.), *Progress and future directions in evaluation: Perspectives on theory, practice, and methods* (*New Directions for Evaluation, No. 76*, pp. 25–39). San Francisco: Jossey-Bass.

Schwandt, T. A. (2003). "Back to the rough ground!": Beyond theory to practice in evaluation. *Evaluation, 9*, 353–364.

Scriven, M. (1994). The final synthesis. *Evaluation Practice, 15*, 367–382.

Scriven, M. (1997). Empowerment evaluation examined. *American Journal of Evaluation, 18*, 165–175.

Scriven, M. (2005a). Empowerment evaluation principles in practice. *American Journal of Evaluation, 26*, 415–417.

Scriven, M. (2005b). Review of *Empowerment evaluation principles in practice*. *American Journal of Evaluation, 26*, 415–417.

Scriven, M. (2017). Empowerment evaluation 21 years later: There is much to admire about empowerment evaluation. *Evaluation and Program Planning, 63*, 138.

Sechrest, L. (1997). Review of *Empowerment evaluation: Knowledge and tools for self-assessment and accountability*. *Environment and Behavior, 29*, 422–426. Retrieved from *www.davidfetterman.com/SechrestBookReview.htm*.

Senge, P. (1994). *The fifth discipline: The art and practice of the learning organization*. New York: Doubleday.

Sette, C. (2016). Participatory evaluation [Web page]. Retrieved from *http://betterevaluation.org/plan/approach/participatory_evaluation*.

Shulha, L. M. (2000). Evaluative inquiry in university–school professional learning partnerships. In V. J. Caracelli & H. Preskill (Eds.), *The expanding scope of evaluation use* (*New Directions for Evaluation, No. 88*, pp. 39–53). San Francisco: Jossey-Bass.

Shulha, L. M. (2010, November). *Participatory evaluation essentials: Highlighting the essential features of participatory evaluation*. Paper presented at the American Evaluation Association Conference, San Antonio, TX.

Shulha, L. M., Whitmore, E., Cousins, J. B., Gilbert, N., & al Hudib, H. (2016). Introducing evidence-based principles to guide collaborative approaches to evaluation: Results of an empirical process. *American Journal of Evaluation, 37*(2), 193–215.

Spivak, G. C. (2008). *Other Asias*. Malden, MA: Blackwell.

Stufflebeam, D. L. (1994). Empowerment evaluation, objectivist evaluation, and evaluation standards: Where the future of evaluation should not go and where it needs to go. *American Journal of Evaluation, 15*, 321–338.

Stufflebeam, D. L., & Shrinkfield, A. J. (2007). *Evaluation theory, models, and applications*. San Francisco: Wiley.

Terborg, J. (1981). Interactional psychology and research on human behavior in organizations. *Academy of Management Review, 6*(4), 569–576.

Tilley, N., & Clarke, A. (2006). Evaluation in criminal justice. In I. F. Shaw, J. C. Greene, & M. M. Mark (Eds.), *The SAGE handbook of evaluation* (pp. 513–536). Thousand Oaks, CA: SAGE.

Topping, K. (1998). Peer assessment between students in colleges and universities. *Review of Educational Research, 68*, 249–276.

Torres, R. T., Padilla Stone, S., Butkus, D., Hook, B., Casey, J., & Arens, S. (2000). Dialogue and reflection in a collaborative evaluation: Stakeholder and evaluation voices. In K. Ryan & L. DeStefano (Eds.), *Evaluation as a democratic process: Promoting inclusion, dialogue, and deliberation* (New Directions for Evaluation, No. 85, pp. 27–38). San Francisco: Jossey-Bass.

UNICEF. (2005). Useful tools for engaging young people in participatory evaluation. Retrieved from *www.artemis-services.com/downloads/tools-for-participatory-evaluation.pdf*.

University of Minnesota. (2016). Ripple effects mapping (REM). Retrieved from *http://blog-ripple-effect-mapping.extension.umn.edu*.

Upshur, C. C., & Barretto-Cortez, E. (1995). What is participatory evaluation (PE)?: What are its roots? *Evaluation Exchange: A Periodical on Emerging Strategies in Evaluation, 1*(3–4). Retrieved from *www.hfrp.org/evaluation/the-evaluation-exchange/issue-archive/participatory-evaluation/what-is-participatory-evaluation-pe-what-are-its-roots*.

U.S. Agency for International Development. (1996). Performance monitoring and evaluation tips: Conducting a participatory evaluation. Retrieved from *http://pdf.usaid.gov/pdf_docs/pnabs539.pdf*.

Veale, J., Morley, R., & Erickson, C. (2001). *Practical evaluation for collaborative services: Goals, processes, tools, and reporting systems for school-based programs*. Thousand Oaks, CA: Corwin Press.

Wagner, M. L., Churl Suh, D., & Cruz, S. (2011). Peer- and self-grading compared to faculty grading. *American Journal of Pharmaceutical Education, 75*(7), Article 130.

Walker-Egea, C. (2015). *A collaborative evaluation of a training program to support organizational competitiveness*. In L. Rodríguez-Campos (Ed.), *Collaborative evaluations in practice: Insights from business, nonprofit, and education sectors*. Scottsdale, AZ: Information Age.

Wandersman, A. (2015). *Getting to outcomes: An empowerment evaluation approach for capacity building and accountability*. Thousand Oaks, CA: SAGE.

Wandersman, A., Imm, P., Chinman, M., & Kaftarian, S. (2000). Getting to outcomes: A results-based approach to accountability. *Evaluation and Program Planning, 23,* 389–395.

Wandersman, A., & Snell-Johns, J. (2005). Empowerment evaluation: Clarity, dialogue, and growth. *American Journal of Evaluation, 26*(3), 421–428.

Weiss, C. H. (1998). *Evaluation* (2nd ed.). Upper Saddle River, NJ: Prentice-Hall.

Wendel, M. L., Prochaska, J. D., Clark, H. R., Sackett, S., & Perkins, K. (2010). Interorganizational network changes among health organizations in the Brazo Valley, Texas. *Journal of Primary Prevention, 31*(1–2), 59–68.

Wharton, J. (2015). Unlocking the potential of collaborative evaluation to increase team performance in a nonprofit. In L. Rodríguez-Campos (Ed.), *Collaborative evaluations in practice: Insights from business, nonprofit, and education sectors.* Scottsdale, AZ: Information Age.

Wilson, R. J., McWhinnie, A. J., Picheca, J. E., Prinzo, M., & Cortoni, F. (2007). Circles of support and accountability: Engaging community volunteers in the management of high-risk sexual offenders. *Howard Journal of Criminal Justice, 46,* 1–15.

Yeh, S. S. (2000). Improving educational and social programs: A planned variation cross-validation model. *American Journal of Evaluation, 21,* 171–184.

Zakocs, R. C., & Edwards, E. M. (2006). What explains community coalition effectiveness?: A review of the literature. *American Journal of Preventative Medicine, 20*(4), 351–361.

Zimmerman, M. A. (2000). Empowerment theory: Psychological, organizational, and community levels of analysis. In J. Rappaport & E. Seldman (Eds.), *Handbook of community psychology* (pp. 20–45). New York: Kluwer Academic/Plenum Press.

Zukoski, A., & Luluquisen, M. (2002). Participatory evaluation: What is it? Why do it? What are the challenges? *Community-Based Public Health Policy and Practice, 5,* 3–8.

Author Index

157

Subject Index

Note. *f*, *n*, or *t* following a page number indicates a figure, a note, or a table.

About the Authors

 David M. Fetterman, PhD, is President and CEO of Fetterman and Associates, an international evaluation consultation firm, and founder of empowerment evaluation. He is also Professor in the School of Business and Leadership at the University of Charleston and Visiting Distinguished Professor of Anthropology at San Jose State University. Dr. Fetterman was a faculty member and administrator at Stanford University for 25 years. Past president of the American Evaluation Association (AEA), he is co-chair of the AEA's Collaborative, Participatory, and Empowerment Evaluation Topical Interest Group. He is a recipient of the Alva and Gunnar Myrdal Evaluation Practice Award for contributions to evaluation practice and the Paul F. Lazarsfeld Evaluation Theory Award for contributions to evaluation theory from the AEA and the Distinguished Scholar Award from the Research on Evaluation Special Interest Group of the American Educational Research Association, among other honors. Dr. Fetterman is the author of 16 books and over 100 chapters, articles, and reports.

 Liliana Rodríguez-Campos, PhD, is Director of the Graduate Certificate in Evaluation and Professor in the Department of Educational and Psychological Foundations at the University of South Florida. She is a former director of the Center for Research, Evaluation, Assessment, and Measurement. Nationally and internationally recognized for her contributions to collaborative evaluation, Dr. Rodríguez-Campos is co-chair of the Collaborative, Participatory, and Empowerment Evaluation Topical Interest Group of the AEA, serves on the board of directors of the Evaluation Capacity Development Group, and is a recipient of the Marcia Guttentag New Evaluator Award from the AEA, among other honors. She has facilitated many training sessions and presented her work in more than 30 countries.

Ann P. Zukoski, DrPH, MPH, has conducted research and evaluation in community-based and public health settings since the 1990s. She leads the Evaluation and Research Team at the Office of Statewide Health Improvement Initiatives of the Minnesota Department of Health. Previously, Dr. Zukoski was a senior research associate at Rainbow Research in Minneapolis, a faculty member in the Department of Public Health at Oregon State University, a senior evaluation associate for the California Public Health Institute, and a senior research associate at the University of California, Berkeley, School of Public Health. She has conducted research and evaluations for national, state, and county agencies, private foundations, and nonprofit organizations. Dr. Zukoski is an acive member of the AEA and has served as president of the Minnesota Evaluation Association. She served as a Peace Corps Volunteer in Berberati, Central African Republic.

About the Contributors

Courtney Baechler, MD, has held leadership roles on the National Prevention Committee for the American College of Cardiology and the Minnesota Department of Health State Prevention of Cardiovascular and Stroke Committee. She has served as a consultant to the State-wide Health Improvement Plan and as chair of the clinical work group for Minneapolis. Dr. Baechler is an author of the *Healthy Lifestyle Guide-line* for the Institute for Clinical Systems Improvement. Dr. Baechler, a preventive cardiologist, is currently Vice President of the Penny George Institute for Health and Healing and the chair of the prevention and wellness clinical service line at Allina Health.

Cate Bosserman, BA, is an evaluator with 5 years of experience promoting community health through partici-patory evaluation. She is currently Community Evaluation Coordinator at the Minnesota Department of Health's Office of Statewide Health Improvement Initiatives. Prior to working at the Department of Health, she was a Research Associate at Rainbow Research, Inc., a mission-driven research and evaluation firm serving community-based organizations, state and local govern-ments, and foundations.

Jill Anne Chouinard, PhD, is Assistant Professor in Educational Research Methodology, School of Education, University of North Carolina at Greensboro. Her main interests are cross-cultural/culturally responsive approaches to research and evaluation, and participatory research and evaluation. Given her interest in utilizing evaluation as a lever for social change, her research also focuses on the relationship between evaluation and public policy. Dr. Chouinard also has extensive experience working on evaluations at the community level in the areas of education and training, social services, health, and organizational learning and change.

Margret Dugan, PhD, is a recipient of the AEA's Marcia Guttentag New Evaluator Award; was honored at the White House for her extensive work in community youth-related research and evaluation; and received the Citizens' Award for Community and Youth Advocacy from the U.S. Department of Health and Human Services for outstanding empowerment evaluation methodology, community engagement, and evidence-based organizational capacity building. She has completed international-, national-, and community-based public health research and evaluations. Dr. Dugan's numerous clients have included the Marin Community Foundation, the San Francisco Foundation, the W. K. Kellogg Foundation, the Hewlett-Packard Foundation, the Metropolitan Life Foundation, the American Heart Association, San Francisco University, Santa Clara University, the U.S. Center for Substance Abuse Prevention, the U.S. Department of Education, the U.S. Department of Health and Human Services, the U.S. Family and Youth Services Bureau, the U.S. Administration on Children, Youth, and Families, and the State of Colorado.

Rita Goldfarb O'Sullivan, EdD, is Associate Professor of Evaluation and Assessment at the University of North Carolina at Chapel Hill, where she teaches graduate courses and established Evaluation, Assessment, and Policy Connections, a unit within the School of Education that conducts local, state, national, and international evaluations. She has specialized in developing collaborative evaluation techniques that enhance evaluation capacity and utilization among educators and public service providers. Dr. O'Sullivan has successfully used collaborative evaluation approaches with public health, education, community development, museum, and family support programs in North Carolina; nonprofit organizations in the southeastern states; and national program initiatives in education and community development. Her publications include *Collaborative Evaluation: Theory and Practice; Practicing Evaluation: A Collaborative Approach;* and *Programs for At-Risk Students: A Guide to Evaluation.* Dr. O'Sullivan has made presentations and conducted evaluation trainings internationally. She served as Director of the AEA Graduate Education Diversity Internship Program and as Secretary/Treasurer of AEA. She is a recipient of the Lifetime Distinguished Service Award from the North Carolina Association for Research in Education and the Robert Ingle Service Award from the AEA.

Jason Ravitz, PhD, is the Educational Outreach Evaluation Manager at Google, focusing on increasing representation in computer science learning. For 12 years, he worked at the Buck Institute for Education conducting research on project-based learning, teacher professional development, and educational technologies.

Rigoberto Rincones-Gómez, PhD, has served nationally and internationally in key leadership roles supporting student success, faculty excellence, scholarly activity, and institutional prominence. He has worked at single and multicampus institutions; for public and private entities; and in urban, suburban, and rural settings. Dr. Rincones-Gómez has coauthored several books, including *Collaborative Evaluations: Step-by-Step, Second Edition;* has designed and facilitated more than 100 workshops; and has published many articles in refereed journals.

Rosalyn Roker, MBA, MA, is Instructor at the University of South Florida and Fellow at the Center for Research Education and Training Enhancement at Florida Agricultural and Mechanical University. She is interested in program evaluation using a collaborative approach. Her research interests include health disparities, particularly the effects of disparities in access, use, and quality of outpatient mental health care services for racial and ethnic minorities across the life course. Her work has been published in several peer-reviewed journals and presented at local and national conferences.

Abraham Wandersman, PhD, is Professor of Psychology at the University of South Carolina, Columbia. He performs research and program evaluation on citizen participation in community organizations and coalitions and on interagency collaboration. Dr. Wandersman is coeditor of three books on empowerment evaluation, and coauthor of several *Getting to Outcomes* accountability books (how-to manuals for planning, implementation, and evaluation to achieve results). He has received the Alva and Gunnar Myrdal Evaluation Practice Award and Outstanding Evaluation Award from the AEA and Award for Distinguished Contribution to Theory and Research from the Society for Community Research and Action. Since 2015, Dr. Wandersman has been involved in the evaluation of several community health initiatives funded by the Robert Wood Johnson Foundation.